ENVIRONMENT AND MAN
VOLUME FOUR

Reclamation

ENVIRONMENT AND MAN: VOLUME FOUR

Titles in this Series

ENVIRONMENT AND MAN
VOLUME FOUR

Reclamation

General Editors

John Lenihan

O.B.E., M.Sc., Ph.D., C.Eng., F.I.E.E., F.Inst.P., F.R.S.E.

Director of the Department of Clinical Physics and Bio-Engineering, West of Scotland Health Boards; Professor of Clinical Physics, University of Glasgow; Chairman of the Scottish Technical Education Council.

William W Fletcher

B.Sc., Ph.D., F.L.S., F.I.Biol., F.R.S.E.

Professor of Biology and Past Dean of the School of Biological Sciences, University of Strathclyde; Chairman of the Scottish Branch of the Institute of Biology; President of the Botanical Society of Edinburgh.

Blackie
Glasgow and London

Blackie & Son Limited
Bishopbriggs
Glasgow G64 2NZ

450/452 Edgware Road
London W2 1EG

International Standard Book Numbers

Paperback 0 216 90128 6
Hardback 0 216 90129 4

Printed in Great Britain by
Thomson Litho Ltd., East Kilbride, Scotland

Background to Authors

Environment and Man: Volume Four

HERBERT L. EDLIN, M.B.E., B.Sc., Dip.For., F.Inst.For., is Publications Officer of the Forestry Commission. An Edinburgh graduate, he has managed Malaysian rubber plantations and New Forest oakwoods, and has travelled widely in Europe, North America and South Africa to study conservation.

DONALD J. HARLEY is Regional Opencast Director in Scotland for the Opencast Executive of the National Coal Board. In the field of opencast coal mining, he has held a wide range of technical and managerial appointments.

J. A. RICHARDSON, M.Sc., Ph.D., M.Inst.P., is Senior Lecturer in Plant Biology at the University of Newcastle. He has worked on botanical problems in reclamation since 1950. He serves on the Northumberland National Park and Countryside Committee, and on the Northern Region Advisory Committee of the Forestry Commission.

JOHN B. McCREATH, B.Sc. (Agric.), N.D.A., is a Senior Agricultural Economist at the West of Scotland Agricultural College, Auchincruive, Ayr. For over twenty years he has specialized in the economic aspects of hill and upland farming. He is a member of the Hill Sheep Development Group of the Scottish Agricultural Development Council.

NINIAN JOHNSTON, Dip. Arch.(Abdn), A.R.I.B.A., A.R.I.A.S., Dip.T.P., joined the staff of Glasgow Corporation Planning Department in 1970. Here he undertook a study for the future planning of the central area of Glasgow, and a study of social deprivation in the East End of the city. From 1973 to 1975 he was Supervisory Planning Officer for the northern area of the city. He is now Projects Manager with the Scottish Tourist Board.

Series Foreword

MAN IS A DISCOVERING ANIMAL—SCIENCE IN THE SEVENTEENTH CENTURY, scenery in the nineteenth and now the environment. In the heyday of Victorian technology—indeed until quite recently—the environment was seen as a boundless cornucopia, to be enjoyed, plundered and re-arranged for profit.

Today many thoughtful people see the environment as a limited resource with conservation as the influence restraining consumption. Some go further, foretelling large-scale starvation and pollution unless we turn back the clock and adopt a simpler way of life.

Extreme views—whether exuberant or gloomy—are more easily propagated, but the middle way, based on reason rather than emotion, is a better guide for future action. This series of books presents an authoritative explanation and discussion of a wide range of problems related to the environment, at a level suitable for practitioners and students in science, engineering, medicine, administration and planning. For the increasing numbers of teachers and students involved in degree and diploma courses in environmental science the series should be particularly useful, and for members of the general public willing to make a modest intellectual effort, it will be found to present a thoroughly readable account of the problems underlying the interactions between man and his environment.

Preface

THE FIRST TWO VOLUMES IN THIS SERIES DEALT WITH THE MATERIAL benefits that man takes from the environment—chiefly energy and food. Volume 3 reviewed the increasing importance of environmental factors in relation to human health. This volume examines another important problem—the reclamation of environmental resources diminished by natural causes, by human intervention or by unexpected interactions between man's activities and natural processes.

The land is sometimes laid waste through no fault of its occupants. The prosperous estate of Culbin, which had survived war and weather for more than five hundred years, was devastated by a storm in 1694 and was, for more than two centuries, Britain's largest desert. Mr. Edlin describes how the area was reclaimed by skilful application of ideas from several disciplines, including botany, meteorology, soil science and forestry. He explains the general principles of this work and shows how they have been applied elsewhere.

In many countries, naked spoil heaps degrade the landscape where coal has been mined. Dr. Richardson shows how these ugly objects can be clothed in vegetation to provide pasture, recreation space and scenery. He draws examples from his own successful work in North-East England, but the methods that he describes are widely applicable and could with advantage be studied in other parts of the world still showing the scars of the industrial revolution.

In some places, coal and other minerals can be won more economically by surface mining than by extraction from under the ground. Opencast mining, now practised on a considerable scale in Britain and North America, is capable of serious damage to the environment. Mr. Harley shows how by careful planning and management the benefits of opencast mining can be fully realized while the environment is restored or, in some instances, distinctly improved.

The ever-growing demand for food encourages efforts to make marginal land more productive. The hills and uplands of Scotland, characterized by poor soil, harsh climate and rugged terrain, illustrate many of the problems of land improvement. Mr. McCreath outlines the scientific and technical principles of this work, with interesting agricultural and economic case histories.

The industrial progress that has ravaged the countryside has left

ix

enduring monuments also in many of the world's great cities—notably in Glasgow, the city of James Watt, Adam Smith and many others whose efforts decisively shaped the pattern of nineteenth-century industry.

The reclamation of the Gorbals between 1957 and 1974 represented one of the most interesting exercises ever undertaken in urban reclamation. Mr. Johnston sketches the background to this project, describes the progress of the work and, assessing the general problem of restoring the decayed inner areas of cities, suggests that Glasgow may have paved the way for new techniques in environmental reclamation.

Our forefathers wrought great deeds in shaping the world in which we live, but they did not appreciate how closely man and his environment are interdependent. The lesson of this book is that we can, by purposeful thought and action, make good some of the errors of the past and avoid environmental disasters in the future.

Contents

CHAPTER ONE

THE CULBIN SANDS

H. L. EDLIN

THE CULBIN SANDS, NOW CLOTHED IN PINEWOODS, ARE AN OBLONG expanse of sand dunes on the coast of the ancient Scottish counties of Moray and Nairn. Though on the eastern side of the country, this coastline actually faces north-west towards the Moray Firth, a wedge-shaped inlet of the North Sea. Situated between the town and river of Nairn, and the mouth of the River Findhorn, the Sands are centred on a point 57° 38′ north in latitude, and 3° 42′ west in longitude. They measure 12 kilometres along the coastline, from south-west to north-east, and average 2½ kilometres in width, inland from the shore. Their total area is some 30 square kilometres or 3000 hectares, and they range in height from sea-level to 30 metres. Their general disposition is illustrated in figure 1.1, which shows the progress of afforestation to 1948.

These Sands are of outstanding interest to conservationists because they are known to have been shifted by a violent storm, or series of storms, in the autumn of A.D. 1694. This caused the sand to overwhelm the sixteen recorded fertile farms and mansion house of an ancient barony. They persisted as a Scottish desert for the next 230 years, though from 1839 onwards there were small-scale attempts to reclaim them. Since 1921 the whole dune system has been afforested by the Forestry Commission (1950), and today it is stabilized and protected by thriving pine forests. The Sands are remarkably homogeneous; they are unbroken by recent agricultural cultivation and nobody lives on them.

Culbin comprises one of the largest aeolian (i.e. wind-borne) deposits formed in recent geological times anywhere in Britain. The mineral composition of the sand, which is remarkably consistent, is made up of

1

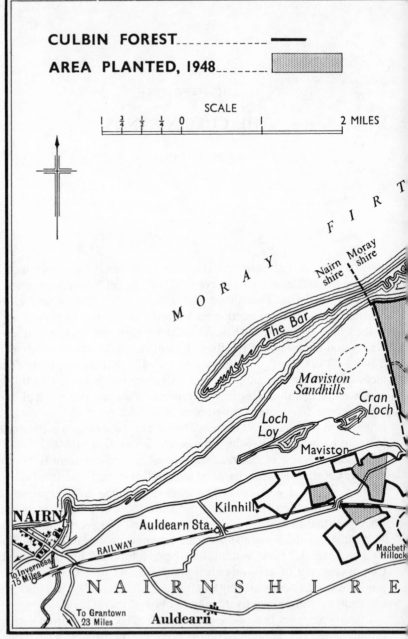

Figure 1.1 Culbin Forest and its surroundings in 1948, showing how afforestation was extended gradually from south-west to north-east (1 mile = 1·6 kilometres).

Lady Culbin

CULBIN SANDHILLS

Binsness

Findhorn

FINDHORN BAY

Hill 99

Kincorth Ho.

Wellhill

w Wood

Snab of Moy

Kintessack

High Wood

Moy Ho.

R. Findhorn

To Elgin 12 Miles

Loanhead

Muirtown

Dyke

FORRES

ead

Brodie Castle

RAILWAY

Knockomie

Brodie Sta.

Blinkbonny

M O R A Y S H I R E

To Grantown 22 Miles

Forestry Commission

78% quartz, 18% felspar, 1% mica, 1% garnet, 1% composite quartz and felspar fragments; the balance of 1% includes magnetite, hornblende, tourmaline, zircon and sphene (Mackie, 1899). This is consistent with their derivation, by erosion, from granites farther inland, but also with several other sources in the form of sandstone rocks and glacial deposits.

The setting

In dealing with Culbin's remarkable complex of sand and seashore, farm, forest and river, we must be wary of accepting any boundaries as fixed and finite. The extent and character of the Culbin Sands has certainly varied through historic time, and indeed is liable to do so today. The modern shoreline is not that of the seventeenth century, which is now virtually impossible to locate.

Today the coast itself is certainly not stable (Steers, 1953); nor is there any consistent and constant trend in the currents that affect its outline. Sometimes there is erosion from the east and sometimes, elsewhere, from the west. Wooden groynes have recently been built at vulnerable points along the beach to cause a build-up of sand and prevent any serious fresh inroads by the sea.

The countryside inland from the Sands forms a part of the famous Laigh (or lowland) of Moray, a region of kindly soil and climate that has been closely settled since early historic times. Though situated in the Highland region of Scotland, it shows marked differences in character from the land to the south. These are aptly expressed by the pithy Scots proverb:

> Speak weel o' the Hielan's
> But *bide* in the Laigh.

The underlying rocks belong to the Upper Old Red Sandstone system and break down to yield fertile easily-worked soils. The climate, influenced by the Gulf Stream on the north, is remarkably mild for the situation, with mean temperatures around 8 °C and remarkably little frost or snow. Since the Laigh lies in the rain shadow of the Grampian mountains to south and west, the rainfall is exceptionally low—only 625 mm annually. Cloudless skies are frequent, and sunshine averages 1300 hours a year. All this contrasts strongly with the true Highland region to the south and west with its hard metamorphic rocks yielding poor soils, high rainfall, harsh winters, and constant cloudiness.

Culbin is in fact part of an isolated stretch of land of high fertility and exceptional climate, which occurs on both sides of the Moray Firth. This Firth is bounded on the north by the Black Isle, a hilly peninsula, and beyond that by the Sutherland Highlands, which form a magnificent scenic feature. On a clear day the eye ranges beyond Ben Wyvis (1045 metres) towards the shapely summits of Morven (704 m) and Maiden Pap (485 m) on the borders of Caithness. To the south, the land rises more gradually towards the distant mass of the high Cairngorms, which reach 1310 m on Ben Macdhui, Scotland's second highest peak, at the centre of the country's largest elevated plateau.

Two rivers that are concerned in the evolution of the Culbin Sands flow in a north-easterly direction from this southern land mass; the Nairn on the west and the Findhorn to the east. Though both flow over exceptionally hard rocks, in times of spate they carry a substantial burden of sand and gravel, mostly derived from the erosion of glacial deposits which are frequent along their upper reaches.

A second major source of sand is the marine erosion of the relatively soft sandstone shoreline, which is illustrated by the high cliffs of the Black Isle, directly opposite to Culbin across the Moray Firth. The immediate hinterland of the Sands, however, shows as its prehistoric coastline, a low raised beach averaging only 6 m above the present sea-level. Between the small towns of Ardersier and Burghead the land to the north of this contour is of a relatively fugitive character, being either swamp or sand dune.

A clue to the former coastline of Culbin is provided by the remarkable seventeenth-century map of Scotland compiled by Gordon of Straloch (Senex, 1721). This shows the village or barony of "Cowbin" placed centrally on a peninsula between the mouths of the Rivers Nairn and Findhorn. This peninsula has an eastward extension towards the present position of "The Bar" offshore (see map). There is a separate bay shown just seaward of Culbin, and the Findhorn estuary has an open mouth instead of the constricted one apparent today. After making due allowance for the small scale (about 1:1,000,000) and the draughtsman's fondness for irregular coastlines, it appears that a visitor to Culbin shortly before its disastrous storm would have found a settlement placed inland from an inlet, no doubt used as a fishing harbour, with a sandspit stretching westwards from the ancient shoreline of hard rock.

The name *Culbin*, if derived from the Gaelic, signifies "nook of the hill", suggesting a sheltered situation below higher ground. The word "bin", from Gaelic *beinn*, head or headland, is applied in this region to any rounded summit. It could have referred to a high sand dune, or a low rocky outcrop.

The barony of Culbin

When an estate has lain below a sand dune for close on 300 years, people are apt to doubt its previous existence, and to refer to it as "legendary". Culbin, however, is well recorded, and the facts have been summarized by Bain (1922). During the twelfth century, Culbin formed part of the extensive lands of one Freskin or Freskinus, probably a Norman or Flemish adventurer, who died in the year 1171. It then passed to his second son, William, laird of the neighbouring estate of Duffus, whose family assumed the title of "de Moravia", the source of today's frequent surname "Murray". A member of this family, Richard of Culbin, is mentioned in an early thirteenth-century charter as the proprietor of Skelboll in Sutherland. The Culbin estate remained in the possession of the de Moravias until about 1400, when their heiress, Egidia, married Thomas Kinnaird of Kinnaird. It continued in the possession of the Kinnairds until soon after its destruction by sand in 1694. The Kirkyard of Dyke nearby holds a monument, dated 1613, erected by the "Laird and Lady of Coolbin"—Walter Kinnaird and Elizabeth Innes, the latter probably a daughter of another famous local family.

During the Covenanting struggles of the seventeenth century, the estate was "wasted" in 1644 by the marauding General Montrose, because its owner failed to show support for King Charles I.

The owner of the estate at the time of the 1694 catastrophe was Alexander Kinnaird, a young man who had recently married the daughter of Rose of Clava. Being ruined financially by the storm, he later petitioned the Scottish Parliament for exemption from cess or land tax. But in 1698 he was obliged to sell what remained of the estate to meet his debts, and both he and his wife died soon afterwards, leaving an heir who had no issue. Subsequent owners of the devastated lands were Duff of Drummuir, from 1698 to about 1733; the Grants of Sheuglie, until 1822; and the Grants of Glenmoriston, who disposed of a major part of the Sands to the Forestry Commission in 1921.

In its prime the estate included sixteen farms, of which only one, called Earnhill, survives. The leased lands covered 3600 acres. The average farm rent is quoted as 200 pounds Scots in money, with forty bolls of wheat, bere, oats and oatmeal in kind. The estate was known as the "Garden" or "Granary" of Moray and, like most estates at that time, had its own mill, the Mill of Dalpottie on the Muckle Burn, to grind grain. There were valuable salmon netting fishings along the foreshore, as well as a harbour for deep-sea fishing craft. The lairds of this prosperous property lived in a square mansion house, built of dressed stone, sheltered by trees, with a garden and orchard nearby.

One of the resources of the estate was marram grass *Ammophila arenaria*, which grew wild on the sandhills, and acted as a stabilizer of the dunes. Tradition asserts that its removal was responsible for the catastrophe, and a few years later the Scottish Parliament passed an act prohibiting the removal of broom, bent (a term that includes grasses of all kinds) and juniper from the seashore. This act is still in force.

The main use to which marram was put was probably thatching, a practice that still continues in Hebridean Islands such as Barra, where straw is scarce. There are, however, a number of crafts that employ marram as their raw material, and as late as the 1920s there was a thriving marram industry at Newborough in Anglesey, which drew its material from local sand dunes. It was used for weaving mats, baskets, hassocks, chair seats, and even whole chairs. Brooms and brushes were made from it, and even sun-hats and sandals (Edlin, 1951). Such craft uses were formerly widespread, and it is possible that Culbin, like Newborough, became a centre of the marram industry, leading to harvesting outstripping the capacity of the grass to make good the loss.

The great storm of 1694

Tradition insists that the whole fertile estate of Culbin was overwhelmed in a single dramatic storm during the "autumn of 1694", though no date has been recorded. Doubts have been expressed on this, and it is indeed unusual for dunes elsewhere to advance by more than a few hundred metres in a whole year. But Scotland is subject from time to time to sustained gales of quite exceptional velocity, which cause widespread windblow amid forests and plantations.

In one such storm, which swept across Central Scotland on 15th January 1968, from south-west to north-east, wind speeds exceeding 120 kilometres per hour were recorded and there were massive blowdowns of trees all the way from Argyll to Fife (Holtam, 1971). It is not hard to imagine such a rare storm striking Culbin in its exposed situation on this northern coast, with devastating results.

An impression of an actual storm on the unstabilized sands, about the year 1900, has been given by John Martin of Elgin, who had evidently been caught in one (Bain, 1922). "The wind," he assures us, "comes rushing down through the openings between the hills, carrying with it immense torrents of sand, with a force and violence almost overpowering. Clouds of sand are raised from the tops of the mounds and are whirled about in the wildest confusion, and fall with the force of hail. Nothing can be seen but sand above and sand below and sand everywhere. The sand blows through the narrow passes as if through a funnel. If you hold out your hand it is immediately filled. You can catch the sand in handfuls. You dare not open your eyes, but must grope your way about as if blindfolded. The whirlwind makes veritable ropes of sand, and the unlucky wight caught in the storm is lashed black and blue by these 'whips of the furies'. St John, the author of *Wild Sport and Natural History in the Highlands*, reported the occasional appearance of human skeletons on the untamed dunes, which suggests that unfortunate travellers may have failed to reach safety."

Bain records a big eastward advance made by unfixed dunes during the first week of May 1920, "when for several days during the occurrence of a westerly gale the sands were set in tremendous motion, running furiously in vast streams or tossed madly in the air. One who was in the vicinity at the time says he could quite realize how the original sandstorm accomplished its fell work in such a short time as is usually attributed to it".

The month of September 1694 is the most probable time for the great storm, for it is said that barley was being harvested when it struck. This would also coincide with the exceptionally low tides connected with the autumn equinox, around September 21, which would expose an exceptionally wide expanse of offshore sand to the drying and blowing action of the wind. Tradition maintains that, prior to the storm, the sea had been gaining on the land, which would account for the disappearance of the westerly headland shown on Gordon's map. The resultant expanse of tide-washed sand, around The Bar, would provide an ideal source for part at least of the sand that blew inland. The rest came from the dunes, which in effect were rolled bodily over the farm land.

At first only fields were invaded. A ploughman had to leave his plough, while reapers left their stooks of barley. When they returned, both plough and barley were buried forever. The drift then advanced upon the village, engulfing the cottages and the laird's mansion. The storm continued through the night, and next morning some of the cottars had to break through the backs of their houses to get out. On the second day of the storm, the people freed their cattle and fled with their belongings to safer ground.

Their flight was obstructed by the River Findhorn, for its mouth had been blocked by drifting sand and its waters rose until it had forced a new passage out to the sea. In so doing it swept away the old village of Findhorn, on the eastern shore, which had been abandoned a short time previously by its inhabitants.

When the people of Culbin returned after the storm, not a trace of their houses was to be seen. All had vanished beneath the sands, which they were powerless to remove. No loss of life is recorded but clearly all their accustomed livelihoods had gone.

The direction of the wind has not been recorded. As discussed later, it may have come from the north-west rather than the south-west, or have varied during the course of the storm.

The Untamed Sands, 1694 to 1921

For the following 230 or so years the Sands remained as an unstable, lifeless wilderness, the plaything of the winds. They held, and indeed still hold, a colossal volume of sand, averaging about 10 metres thick over an area of some 30 square kilometres. Looking back it is surprising that nobody found this a useful resource, or alternatively declared the Sands to be a national monument and hence untouchable for all time! Having nothing to offer in the way of sport or fodder for farm stock, they were visited only by the odd longshore fisherman or curious traveller in search of the picturesque.

The system was basically unstable, and the situation and height of the tallest dunes changed from year to year. In 1950 the highest dune, still unplanted, near the eastern end of the system, was known as "Lady Culbin". Its height was 30 metres, and it had a long gentle slope up from the seashore on the west, and a very abrupt one down towards the Findhorn estuary on the east. Sand grains were blown up the gentle slope to the crest, by the prevailing south-west winds. Grains that got carried over the top fell sharply down into the sheltered lee, moving in little "rivers" as their weight made the crest unstable. As a result the whole dune was steadily advancing eastwards. Ovington (1950) found that vertical poles, two metres high, were buried in six weeks, though he does not state the distance or wind speeds involved. Winds with a westerly element blow for 46% of the time at Nairn nearby, comparable with 26% for all other directions; the balance of 28% consists of calm spells.

Overall, the dunes were slowly but steadily transported to the Findhorn estuary, which they tended to block. But the Findhorn inevitably restored its seaward channel at every ebb tide and carried the deposited material out to sea. It has been suggested that easterly currents then returned it to the Culbin beaches, where it was blown ashore again and so circulated indefinitely. This could occur, but alternatively the sand might be carried eastwards to help build up other dune systems about 13 kilometres long, on and beyond the shores of Burghead Bay. The actual course taken no doubt varied, depending on tidal flows and the strength of river and sea currents.

Studies and photos by His Majesty's Geological Survey for Scotland, apparently made about 1910, reveal considerable diversity in the character of these mobile dunes. Some formed a classical crescent, with low horns moving to leeward in advance of a higher centre. Others built up into hummocks. Mobile dunes, free of all vegetation, sometimes advanced over lower fixed ones carrying marram grass. Elsewhere the wind would blow out odd hollows and valleys, and everywhere it left ripple marks like those seen on a wet beach. I was fortunate, in 1947, to see something of this fascinating pattern before it was finally halted by the completion of afforestation in 1954.

From time to time the wind would move the dunes clear of the original land surface, though only over small areas. About the year 1820 the ruins of the mansion house were exposed, only to vanish again beneath a fresh drift. At times the furrows of ploughed fields have been revealed and so has the old bed of the River Findhorn. Hollows between the dunes often revealed buried beaches, with a bed of rounded shingle intermixed with sea shells. Occasionally these hollows flooded after rains, forming temporary "winter lakes" that attracted waterfowl.

Antiquarians seeking relics in these exposed hollows made some curious hauls. Extensive hoards of flint arrow heads, scrapers and axes showed that the beaches were inhabited in Stone Age times. Roman coins and bronze jewellery linked the site with Celtic times, while the mediaeval and recent periods were represented by iron nails, fish hooks, fragments of pottery, and coins of various centuries from various lands, suggesting sea-borne trade. The drifting sands had both preserved these relics and checked the vegetation that usually conceals them.

The local source of the fresh sand that maintained the system was, and remains, a constant and reliable one. At every low tide the extensive flats around The Bar dry out to the point at which any on-shore wind, if blowing with reasonable force, picks up individual grains of sand and carries them inland. This process continues until halted by the next tide. It is aided by the constant sunshine and low rainfall of the region, which helps the beaches to dry quickly. The supply of sand to the flats, at high tide, is the work of rivers and ocean currents.

Early afforestation, 1839 to 1921

Though the main expanse of the Sands, on the seaward side, remained untouched, a good deal of tree planting was carried out, with varied results, on their inland fringe. In 1839 a Mr Grant of Kincorth, at the eastern end of the sandy wastes, planted a belt of Scots pine and broad-leaved trees to shelter his mansion. This flourished and encouraged his neighbours to follow suit. A Major Chadwick established plantations at Binsness close to the Findhorn estuary, after planting marram grass to stabilize the sand. Other plantations were made on the Dalvey estate near Kintessack, on the Brodie property close to Bankhead, and in the centrally-placed Low Wood and High Wood of the Moy Estate, near Snab of Moy. Most of the resulting timber was clear-felled during the 1939–45 war, when steam sawmills were set up to convert the logs to planks.

A similar project on the Maviston Sandhills, lying more exposed and nearer to the seashore on the west, proved ill-fated. After the pines had become well established and had reached heights around 10 metres, they were approached, about the year 1910, by a vast moving dune. This engulfed them completely, piling up sand to a height above the tree tops. When it eventually moved on, only the dead leafless skeletons of trees remained.

Elsewhere occasional trees have been known to survive partial, though not complete, burial. A dune that encroached on the Low Wood, but became stable, gave rise to some very oddly-shaped pine trunks. Normally a tree trunk tapers evenly upwards, but these half-buried stems tapered away both upwards and downwards, being stoutest at the new surface of the sand, and thinner above and below.

It was apparent that piecemeal efforts by half a dozen proprietors, each tackling a small section of the Sands, could never succeed in taming the main drifting mass, which was being constantly replenished by the sea. Fortunately the Forestry Commission came forward with larger resources and was able to acquire, by stages, virtually the whole of the Sands, by purchases from the estates of Moy, Brodie, Dalvey, Binsness, and Loch Loy near Maviston, between 1921 and 1954.

The conquest of the Sands, 1921 to 1954

The newly-formed Forestry Commission, established in 1919, approached the Culbin Sandhills as part of its remit to increase home production of timber, make good use of otherwise waste lands, and promote rural employment. Culbin was a challenge, but the Commission's small staff of expert foresters included men who had tackled similar projects overseas. Obviously the dangerous seaward side of the Sands must be fixed first, and work began at the Nairnshire–Morayshire boundary, which was then the limit of the land acquired. The plan was to work from south-west to north-east.

The classic method of fixing mobile dunes has always been the planting of marram grass *Ammophila arenaria*, or similar tough vegetation. This was pursued for the first ten years, though with only limited success. Marram is an exceptionally sturdy, greenish-grey perennial grass that forms smooth, stout stems from 75 to 150 centimetres long. These spring from stout jointed far-creeping stolons that bear frequent root clusters. The long leaves are grooved and become inrolled in dry weather, a mechanism that restricts water loss on the dry sites where marram grows. It bears long plume-like flower heads, and scatters plentiful seed.

Naturally resistant to sea salt, sunshine, and drought, marram shows a remarkable defence against drifting sand. When sand piles up over it, it grows up through the new surface layers. Its long stems maintain contact with the flexible stolon system, whose roots tap water held in the dune at lower levels. The marram system holds together even when a blow-out occurs and the bare stolons become exposed.

Marram spreads naturally by blown seed and wandering shoots. It can also be readily propagated by cutting offshoots and setting them deeply in the sand. This process was adopted at Culbin to take marram out into the completely bare zones near the sea front. Tufts were pulled up from dense marram groups elsewhere, and planted in small holes in the blown sand, at a distance of 0·8 metre apart. Little growth occurs in the first year, but provided the grass is not completely blown out or too deeply covered by fresh sand, it spreads readily thereafter. A moderate influx of sand seems to stimulate its growth, possibly because it brings with it fresh nutrients. Tree planting was usually delayed until three years after planting the marram grass, to give the latter time to become well established.

The value of marram grass for reducing wind speeds close to ground level was investigated by Salisbury (1952) on the Braunton Dunes in Devon. He found that at 60 centimetres above ground level the marram reduced wind speeds by close on half, as compared with speeds on bare sandy dunes nearby. The range on the open dunes was 16 to 32 kilometres per hour, averaging 24; the comparable figures for marram-covered dunes were 10 to 16 km/h, averaging 12 km/h. Close to the critical point of ground level, however, marram reduced wind speeds to only one quarter of those found in the open. At 5 centimetres up, wind speeds range from 11 to 16 km/h, averaging 12 on open dunes; but were only 2 to 3 km/h, averaging 2·5 where the marram grew. It is, of course, the ground-level air current that sets the sand grains in motion. This slowing down of air movement explains why the marram "fixes" the surface fairly effectively, but it is apt to bend before the wind, allowing the air to filter between its slender blades. The more rigid brushwood thatch, which was brought in later, does not bend in this way.

On level ground, a wind speed of only 1·6 km/h is enough to set dry sand grains in motion. Higher speeds are needed to cause them to ascend slopes. The necessary impetus is often applied by one grain flying a short distance, then striking and accelerating another. A pocket of still air, or at least a hollow in which air currents have no single directional trend, is needed to arrest such movement. Thatching provides such "cells".

Tree Planting

Experience elsewhere suggested that pines were the only trees likely to thrive under the prevailing conditions of dry sandy salty soil, low rain-fall, and sunny summers. No other trees have been used on any consider-able scale. The native Scots pine *Pinus sylvestris* had been shown to thrive in the private estate plantings; it can adapt to a wide range of sites, but as it is a low timber-volume producer, its use was in practice confined to the poorer dry zones on the lower dunes. For the main crop on the upper sandhills, reliance was placed on a rather unlikely species, the Corsican pine *P. nigra*, variety *maritima*. It was reasoned correctly that it could thrive in this exceptionally dry and sunny district, though it fails in wetter districts so far north. Damp patches of shingle were planted with the lodgepole pine *P. contorta*, on the reasoning that, as it was a coastal tree in British Columbia, it should do well beside this Scottish sea. It has proved a remarkable success, and these Culbin plantings have pioneered the way for the widespread use of this valuable quick-growing pine, which tolerates poor soils, elsewhere in the Highlands. Two seashore pines that were tried on a modest scale and then abandoned, as they had clearly been taken outside their climatic range, were the maritime pine *P. pinaster*, from the Mediterranean, and the Monterey pine *P. radiata*, from California.

All the pines were raised from seed in a large nursery established at Newton, near Elgin. They were grown as seedlings for two years, reaching a height of about ten centimetres. They were then transplanted to make them form bushy root systems, well adapted to take up water and so survive the shock of transplanting to dry sand. In their "transplant year" in the nursery, the seedlings grew only about four centimetres taller, but their roots expanded markedly; the result was a "well-balanced" transplant, with a large root system in relation to its short top.

The actual planting of the dunes was done in spring, a season when increasing warmth ensured the start of root growth, and hence a quick firm contact with the water-holding soil. A surprising feature of these dry dunes is that there is nearly always water a few centimetres below the surface. The dry layer at the top, a few centimetres deep, helps to con-serve the moisture below; there is a break in the capillary attraction of the water where the dry sand begins.

The usual planting distance was 1·4 metres each way, rather close by current standards. This spacing required approximately 5000 trees per hectare. All these were planted by hand, using a modified garden spade, called the "Schlich" planting spade, after its German inventor; this has a straight shank and a straight blade with curved edges tapering to a point. With this tool the worker cut a deep notch in the sand, inserted the tree's roots, and then stamped the sand firm around the whole tree. One man planted a thousand small trees daily.

Only a modest proportion of the Sands was afforested each year. Overall, thirty-three years were devoted to planting 3000 hectares, an average of less than 100 hectares annually. This was deliberate policy, since it was felt safest to proceed gradually from the south-west of the Sands towards the north-east, stabilizing successive bands and providing shelter for young trees planted to leeward of older ones. This also suited the Commission's overall policy of long-term sustained employment. Unemployment was for long a major problem in this district, as changes in fishing and farming practices threw up a surplus of labour.

Under the Culbin conditions, marram grass proved over the years to be an uncertain and unreliable stabilizer of sand. Strong winds swept aside its slender stems and leaves, and exposed slopes were apt to "blow out". The pines amidst it might have their roots exposed, so that they died of drought, or alternatively they got smothered where sand piled up. On one particularly bad stretch the trees grew only two metres in twenty-five years, against a normal performance of ten metres.

Thatching
About 1940, therefore, the change was made to the practice of thatching the dunes with brushwood (figure 1.2). The thatch was secured from two

Figure 1.2 Thatching a mobile dune with pine stems imported from a neighbouring forest. When spread on the bare sand, the thatch will check wind speeds at ground level and so halt movement of sand grains.
Tom Weir

sources—the pruning of side branches from the few plantations that had become established, and "cleaning", or weeding-out of unwanted woody trees such as birch, in other forests farther inland. Substantial quantities were needed, up to 100 metric tonnes per hectare. The imported thatch was brought in by lorry. The final stage of transport over the soft roadless dunes was achieved by loading it on large sledges drawn by a small crawler tractor (figure 1.3). The stems, still carrying leaves or needles, were laid down with their butts toward the prevailing wind, giving a uniform surface covering that was well placed to deflect the air currents. In very exposed places the thatch was held down by wires fixed to pegs. The trees were planted through the thatch, as close as possible to the desired square spacing, and left to grow up through it as it slowly decayed.

Thatch proved an effective stabilizer because, like the marram, it slowed up the air currents at ground level to a point at which they could no longer disturb sand grains and set them in dangerous motion. It created a microclimate of calm air less than half a metre deep, but that sufficed. The decaying leaves and branchwood also aided the tree crop by supplying a small but valuable quantity of humus to the surface soil. This proved a good rooting medium. Along with it came minute but critically important amounts of mineral nutrients.

Figure 1.3 Dune fixation at Culbin. A crawler tractor draws a sledge laden with pine-branch thatch to the fixation area.
Forestry Commission

Thatching and planting went forward steadily until 1954, progress being sometimes limited by the supply of thatch. At length the last free dune, near the mouth of the Findhorn, was mastered, and all that remained for the sand-fixers to do was to watch for odd blow-outs and re-thatch them (figure 1.4). As the pines grew taller they provided their own protection against the wind, replacing the deteriorating thatch. Eventually they reached the stage when they too contributed branchwood, fallen needles and therefore nutrients to the forest soil, as discussed later. By 1975, twenty years after the last dune was planted, and fifty-five years after the process began, the whole of the Sands carried a self-sustaining pinewood (figure 1.5).

Characteristics of the dune forest

The forest that has developed from the planting of the fixed sand shows few marked differences from the general run of pine forests in the neighbouring lowlands. After a few years of slow growth, averaging only ten to fifteen centimetres in height annually, growth accelerates to around forty centimetres a year. This is maintained for a space of sixty or seventy

Figure 1.4 Corsican pines ten years after planting on dunes partially fixed with marram grass. Thatch has recently been added to a "blow-out" patch in the foreground.
R. M. Adam

years, giving ultimate heights of about twenty-five metres. About ten years from the time of planting, the branches of the trees, planted 1·4 metres apart, meet. Thereafter mutual competition results in the formation of a continuous canopy of foliage. This is obviously of great value in checking further movement of the sand by the wind, for it creates a calm zone near ground level.

An important aftermath of canopy closure is the progressive dying-off of the lower branches, which become overshaded and cease to play an active part in the tree's photosynthetic nutrition. Gradually these branches break away and their debris is added to the steady fall of dead pine needles. The lifespan of an evergreen pine needle varies between three and six years. Once canopy has been formed the numbers and weights of withered needles are similar to the numbers and weights of fresh needles formed annually. A mat of leaf litter therefore builds up on the forest floor, and forms a further protection against any movement of the sand. The litter in this layer gradually breaks down and returns its mineral nutrients to the soil. But the layer as a whole remains intact, being replenished annually through fresh leaf-fall.

When the tree crop is between twenty and twenty-five years old, the

Figure 1.5 Boundary between twenty-year-old Scots pine plantation (right) and six-year-old Corsican pine plantation (left). Note remains of pine-branch thatch used to stabilize the sand, and the invasion by low bushes of broom.
Forestry Commission

forester intervenes to thin the trees out. This is done to give survivors more growing space, but as only a fraction of the crop, never more than 25%, is taken out at one time, the protecting canopy remains substantially intact. At Culbin, thinning began about 1944, in crops established around 1922, and has proceeded steadily since. There is a regular harvest of useful poles that find a ready market locally for fencing, chipboard manufacture, pulpwood for paper making and, in their larger sizes, sawmill timber. The rate of thinning is regulated to match the rate of growth, and each section, or *compartment*, of the forest is dealt with in turn, on a cycle of four or five years.

Eventually, at an age around seventy years, each compartment will be considered mature, and steps will be taken to regenerate it by replacing the fully grown trees with younger ones. The forester has two options here. He can either make "clear fellings" and replant them, or he can thin out the older trees and allow young seedlings to grow up as more and more light reaches the forest floor. This replacement stage has not yet been reached at Culbin, but obviously no large clearings will ever be made, as they might allow the wind to gain a hold once more on the uncertain foundation of blown sand.

A system of rides, i.e. unmetalled roads, was laid out through the forest as soon as planting began. These provide access routes for management and the extraction of logs, first as relatively small poles from the thinnings, and later as large logs suitable for the sawmill. The carpet of fallen pine needles, resting on the dry freely-draining sand, provides a reasonably firm surface for this occasional traffic. Logs are drawn out to the rides, from the points where trees are felled in the plantations, by a tractor. This is equipped with a winch at the rear, and this raises the ends of the logs clear of the ground, so reducing the tractive effort required and avoiding damage to the ground surface.

The rides also serve as fire-breaks, and have proved their worth on the few occasions when forest fires have occurred at Culbin. They permit quick access by fire-fighters, and provide base lines along which the spread of an outbreak can be checked.

Because of this high fire danger, and the fragile character of the environment generally, it has not proved practicable to allow general public access to this forest, though limited exploration is permitted on foot. The Forestry Commission has established an information centre at Cloddymoss, where visiting parties, particularly groups from schools, can be received for controlled excursions.

From the economic standpoint Culbin is well placed for the profitable growth of timber. The soil, though odd, has proved fertile enough for tree crops. Over a sufficient span of time, trees return the bulk of the nutrients they need to the ground, in leaf litter or as branchwood. Access over the freely-draining sand is good, and established markets for timber lie close at hand. The land itself was bought cheaply, having no alternative use, and the labour-intensive business of thatching the dunes was carried out when wage levels were, both actually and comparatively, very low. In the mid-nineteen-twenties, for example, an able-bodied man earned £1·50 *a week* or 3p per hour! A perpetual asset has therefore been created at moderate cost.

Experimental work to increase production has followed two lines. A "deficiency garden" has been set up, with the advice of the Macaulay Institute for Soil Research at Aberdeen, to demonstrate the principal nutritional deficiencies of the relatively poor sandy soils. This has pointed the way to the regular application of nitrogenous fertilizers. A group of species plots has also been established to show how different trees may fare in these exceptional surroundings. Bird life in this young forest has also been intensively investigated by zoologists from the Forestry Department of Aberdeen University.

Soil changes following afforestation

The physical structure of the dunes, now fixed by the pinewoods, is remarkable for its homogeneity. Analyses made by Ovington (1950) showed that 98% of the mass of unplanted dunes consist of "coarse sand", i.e. sand with particles within the limits 200 to 2000 micrometres (μm). The remainder comprises 1·5% of "fine sand" (20–200 μm), plus about 0·5% of "clay", with particle sizes below 2 μm. The "silt" fraction, between "fine sand" and "clay" is scarcely represented at all. Samples taken at various depths from 1·3 cm to 120 cm present the same picture. Following afforestation, there was a slight but significant increase in the percentage of "fine sand" present in the upper soil layers and, twenty years after planting, it had risen to 3% on average. Possibly the more stable forest soil, protected from the wind, is able to hold more of the finer particles than the open wind-swept dune surfaces can do; some sand still blows in.

Ovington's researches were directed to evaluating changes following afforestation, and he concentrated inquiries on three situations. One was the open unplanted dune, the second was a ten-year-old plantation, and the third a plantation aged twenty years (figures 1.3, 1.4 and 1.5). In the ten-year-old plantation the trees were only two metres high; the foliage of adjacent trees was only just beginning to meet, and no litter layer had yet developed on the surface of the sand. By contrast, in the twenty-year-old plantation the trees were six metres high, and their crowns had met to form a continuous canopy. Pine needles and other organic debris falling from this had created a continuous litter layer that lay superficially on the top of the sand. He observed little mixing between the organic and the mineral layers, but could detect the start of podzolization. This implies the leaching-out of minerals from the upper soil layers through the action of acids derived from the litter. Already the upper sand zones were paler than those below, a key feature of podzolized soils.

After twenty years growth, pine tree roots had penetrated to depths of 122 cm, but most were concentrated in the upper 40 cm.

Chemical analyses showed that the development of the tree crop was causing a remarkable increase in the mineral nutrients present in the surface soil, offset by a decrease at the lower levels. It appeared that tree roots were removing certain nutrients from the lower layers to nourish the foliage. Leaf fall was then returning them to the soil, but concentrated at its surface. For example, the concentration of phosphorus, expressed as milligrams of P_2O_5 per litre of soil volume, averaged 10 below the bare dune and the ten-year plantation. Under the twenty-year plantation it had risen to 20 in the surface layers but had fallen to 5 below depths of half a metre. Similar changes in distribution were found for magnesium, potassium, nitrogen, carbon, calcium and manganese. The concentration of available sodium, however, remained unaffected by tree growth; sodium is here steadily replenished by salt blown in from the sea.

The average pH of the sand in all three situations was 5·0, or slightly acid. It increased to 4·0, or markedly acid, in the humus layer under the twenty-year plantation. These figures are lower than those of many dunes. Where sea shells are abundant, their calcium carbonate makes the dunes alkaline. During the summer months, the water content in the soil below the twenty-year plantation was markedly lower than that found elsewhere. This was no doubt due to the transpiration loss caused by the tree's foliage, plus evaporation of rain from tree crowns. The unplanted dunes, though dry at the surface, held substantial quantities of moisture just below it. Representative figures for moisture present to a depth of 125 cm in June, were 70,000 grams per square metre for an unplanted area, but only 26,000 below twenty-year-old trees. The shallow litter layer below these trees does, however, intercept and retain substantial quantities of rain falling in summer showers. This is available to tree roots but is difficult to evaluate.

Changes in ground flora

As might be expected in such a specialized habitat, the number of plant species is limited. Moving dunes carry no flora at all and, on the fixed ones, marram grass *Ammophila arenaria* is everywhere dominant. It remains a common feature in plantations up to ten years old, thriving in the spaces between the trees. Thereafter it is gradually shaded out and, in plantations aged twenty years and over, it becomes quite rare. Its associated grasses, such as *Agrostis tenuis, A. stolonifera* and *Holcus lanatus,* have greater tolerance of shade and linger longer, as does the sand sedge *Carex arenaria.* Bushes of broom *Sarothamnus scoparius* grow vigorously in the younger plantations, probably from seed introduced along with the thatching material. But as the trees get taller and close canopy, the broom is shaded out and only occasional bushes persist along ride sides. Among the smaller plants, the red-flowered sheep's sorrel *Rumex acetosella* follows a similar course.

Mosses become remarkably abundant. Their demands on nutrients, light, and water are low, and here they compete effectively with higher plants. Two species of *Polytrichum,* namely *P. juniperum* and *P. piliferum,* appear as soon as the surface sand ceases to move. Indeed, they seem able to help in its fixation, by forming close mats on the surface and growing up through any casual sand accretions. These moss mats persist through the young plantation stage and are not suppressed by the shade of taller crops later. Other common mosses in established pinewoods are *Rhacomitrium fasciculare, Brachythecium purum, Hypnum cupressiforme* and *Hylocomium splendens.* Lichens, which also make low demands on their environment, become frequent. Locally the ground cover of the older pinewoods consists almost entirely of moss and lichen, plus pine needle litter and debris of dead twigs, buds, flowers and cones, with no higher plants in evidence.

Fungi, which feed on organic matter and bring about its decay, are virtually absent from the unplanted dunes. But several species have been introduced along with the thatching material, and have become well established in the older woods. Some are believed to form active mycorrhizal associations with the pine trees, and so aid their nutrition. One genus involved is *Boletus,* and *B. granulatus, B. scaber,* and *B. elegans* are all present. So is the scarlet flycap *Amanita muscaria,* which has conspicuous scarlet-and-white toadstools, and is known to form mycorrhizal associations with the roots of birch trees (*Betula* species). As dead timber becomes available, timber-rotting fungi such as *Chlorosplenium aeruginosum* make their appearance; these also were probably first introduced on the thatching material, though they could have arrived as wind-borne spores from woods farther inland.

The only broadleaved tree to appear with any frequency at Culbin is birch, usually the hairy birch *Betula pubescens.* It occasionally establishes itself by natural seeding on ridesides and waste grounds. The tough woody creeping willow *Salix repens* grows in sands close to the shore, as a prostrate shrub.

Faunal changes

The bare mobile dunes were remarkable for the absence of birds and beasts, and even of invertebrate creatures. They provided neither sustenance nor shelter, and visitors remarked on their silence and absence of bird song. As the plantation developed, they were gradually invaded by the creatures that are characteristic of neighbouring pinewoods in the Laigh of Moray; some came in to feed and others, such as wood pigeons, simply to rest and nest. Certain species of tits have become permanently resident, finding their food in the insect life that has developed as the plantations have grown taller. One of the commonest of these is the little brown-and-grey coal tit *Parus ater*, which searches for insects, eggs and pupae in bark crevices the whole year round. Another newcomer is the crested tit *P. cristatus*, once very rare but now spreading towards the coast from its long-established haunts in the upper Spey Valley. Soon after the pine tree cones began to mature, the seed-eating crossbill *Loxia curvirostra* moved in from adjacent pinewoods.

Pine seeds have also attracted small rodents such as wood mice, and the truly arboreal red squirrel *Sciurus vulgaris*. The dainty roe deer *Capreolus capreolus*, which is native to the pinewoods of this region, has found its way to the shelter of the Culbin plantations too.

Insects peculiar to pinewoods inevitably appeared at an early stage. Some flew, others were carried in on thatching material, or were even blown in by high winds. One that eventually increased to plague proportions was the pine looper moth *Bupalus piniarius*. This mates in late spring, and its numerous eggs hatch into green caterpillars that feed voraciously on pine needles. It can defoliate whole trees, which seldom recover. The outbreak was checked by the aerial spraying of the affected areas with a DDT insecticide, applied in midsummer at the height of the insects' feeding season. A high percentage kill was achieved, and there has been no serious recurrence. The moth is still present in considerable numbers, but natural enemies now appear to keep it under control.

Was Culbin really a menace?

It has often been said, in justification of the Forestry Commission's action in reclaiming the Culbin Sands by afforestation, that they formed a "menace" to the fertile agricultural lands that lie beside them.

On the face of things, this thesis appears hard to support. Since the original disaster of 1694, the Sands have encroached only marginally on the farms to the south-east. The movement of the dunes has been north-easterly, parallel to the coastline. On reaching the Findhorn estuary, the sand has been blown into it and washed out to sea on the ebb tides. It may, on one theory, even circulate and be blown in again from The Bar to make successive, but harmless, round trips!

But, so long as the dunes stood poised above the neighbouring farms, there was always a fear that they might one day change direction. This might well have occurred on the night of 31st January 1953, when a fantastic storm, blowing from the north-west, struck the north-east shoulder of Scotland. Culbin lay directly in its path, and there were widespread falls of grown timber on neighbouring estates, particularly that of Lethen, just inland. Little damage was, however, suffered by the Culbin plantations, because they had not yet reached the critical height at which trees were overthrown. The Culbin trees, being young, were still supple as well as relatively short; they swayed before the wind, but did not break.

The fixation of the dunes was, by 1953, virtually complete, and there was no substantial area of bare sand left at the mercy of this gale. Had things been otherwise, it is reasonable to suppose that a substantial volume of sand would have been carried south-east by the gale, to overwhelm neighbouring farmland.

The unusual direction of this gale, at right angles to the prevailing wind, may throw some light on the 1694 catastrophe. We can assume that, at that date, the prevailing south-west winds had built up a series of dunes parallel to the coast, which were moving regularly in the same direction. These would pose no apparent threat to the estate that lay beside them; in fact, the higher they grew, the more shelter they would give from cold north winds.

But a storm of the same intensity as the January 1953 gale, coming from the same north-west direction, could move the sand swiftly inland over a long front, probably the whole twelve-kilometre length of the present Culbin shore. It has been aptly said that: "The prevailing wind does not *always* prevail." A strong "cross" wind, of sufficient duration, could wreak tremendous harm. If it continued for several days, the supply of sand from the beaches would be reinforced over an unusually long front at each successive low tide; at a time of maximum tidal fall, a very broad beach would be exposed. In round figures, sand would blow in from a north-western coastline of 12 km, instead of south-western one of only 2½ km. It might also descend from high dunes towards lower farmland.

Steers (1953) rejects the theory of a sudden inundation in favour of a series of slow infiltrations of sand spread over many years. But he assumes that the sand must have blown "eastwards". If, instead, the disastrous storm blew from the north, it could have moved a sufficiently large volume of sand over the much shorter distance involved, in a significantly shorter time. He also appears to regard a wind of 100 km/h, maintained for several hours, as a near-impossible event. But Holtam (1971) shows that such speeds were in fact maintained for over seven hours, over a large area of Argyll, during the gale of 15th January 1968. Though Culbin was outside the main area then involved, a speed of 74 km/h was recorded at Lossiemouth nearby.

In the present century, the threat to the lands neighbouring Culbin was even greater than in the past, owing to the larger mass of loose sand that had accumulated. Afforestation was therefore a safeguard that can be fully justified in the interests of sound land use, affecting both farming and forestry.

Duneland reclamation elsewhere

The Forestry Commission's successful achievement at Culbin has been repeated at other dunelands along the British coasts, but only on a lesser scale. There are two reasons for this. Dunes extensive enough to form sites sufficiently large for an economic forest unit are few and far between, though smaller systems are frequent along many stretches of coastline. Then, at the few larger dune complexes, there is keen competition from other forms of land use, which often have a stronger claim.

One alternative use is for nature conservation, and several dunes have very properly been given a special status, as Nature Reserves or Sites of Special Scientific Interest, by the Nature Conservancy Council. Another demand is for public recreation, sometimes as golf links but elsewhere for bathing beaches or open walking country. A less attractive, but unfortunately essential use, is as military training grounds, aircraft bombing rangers, or sites for the manufacture of dangerous explosives. Dunes attract organizations who want to blow things up, because they are uninhabited and also easily manipulated. The construction of oil rigs or nuclear power installations is another potential use of the lonely beaches or headlands on which dunes are found. Airfields have claimed many of the flatter stretches.

In reviewing the reclaimed areas, a fact that becomes apparent is that no two dune systems are alike. The direction of the coast and its currents, the lie of the land, and the presence or absence of sand-bearing rivers nearby, all affect the way in which the dunes are built up. At any one place, records show that the pattern varies from time to time, with the sea sometimes gaining and at other times giving way to the land. Static situations are virtually unknown.

North-east Scotland

Proceeding clockwise along the Scottish coast from Culbin, an extensive pinewood known as Roseisle, part of the Laigh of Moray Forest, fringes the coast between Findhorn and Burghead. With a total extent of 1600 hectares, it has a shore-line of six kilometres, lying along the crescent-shaped Burghead Bay. This coast faces north at its westerly extremity, but swings round to an easterly direction close to the town of Burghead. Prevailing westerly winds carry sand, which probably originates as material borne seawards by the Findhorn River, east towards this curving beach. It has been blown inland to form a sandy waste. At one time, sand frequently choked the Burghead branch railway, which had to be protected by screens.

These dunes have been successfully afforested with Scots and Corsican pines. Now that these trees have grown tall and fire risk has diminished, the Forestry Commission has been able to encourage public access to the beach by the provision of a car park and picnic places. Already roe deer, squirrels and capercaillie grouse have appeared in the new Roseisle pinewoods.

The coast east of Burghead is rocky, but beyond Lossiemouth, some 15 km eastwards, its character changes to a low sandy shore, this time facing north-east. Between Lossiemouth and Kingston at the mouth of the River Spey, the Lossie pinewoods extend along the coast for 7 km, covering wastes once known as the Links of Innes. Their total extent is 600 hectares. The sand that built up these low links probably originates in the outflow of the large and powerful River Spey. Some probably comes from the rapid erosion of the soft conglomerate sandstone rocks inland around Fochabers, where steep-sided gullies run between narrow ridges known as *drumlachs*.

Most of the Buchan coast is steep and rocky, but near Newburgh, between the River Ythan and the North Sea, there is an extensive dune system known as the Sands of Forvie; they follow the coast for five kilometres and extend inland for two. Forvie, like Culbin, is a "buried barony". The traveller Pennant, in his *First Tour*, recorded that: "The parish of Forvie is now entirely overwhelmed with sand, except two farms. It was in 1660 all arable land, now covered with shifting sands, like the deserts of Arabia, and no vestiges remain of any buildings except a small fragment of a church." Gordon of Straloch (Senex, 1721) plots it as a township called "Forvern". Today it is a maze of shifting sandy hillocks, broken by occasional marshes and lochans where gulls, terns and divers resort to breed each spring, under the protection appropriate to a national Nature Reserve.

Fife

Tentsmuir Forest, in Fife, is now the Commission's second largest sand dune woodland, with an area of 1600 hectares, all in one oblong block. It stands in the easternmost corner of the county, where the Firth of Tay meets the open North Sea, 11 km north of St Andrews. It borders the Firth for about three kilometres, and the sea for five, and lies close to sea-level, with only occasional sandy hillocks rising for ten metres or so above it. This almost level sandspit originates from the deposition of sand carried downstream by the Tay, which is actively eroding rocks and glacial deposits in its upper reaches. The Tay also forms sandbanks in its main course, some close to Dundee, some north of Tayport and others far out to seaward, east of Tentsmuir.

The situation at Tentsmuir contrasts markedly with that at Culbin, because here the prevailing wind blows off-shore. The sand tends to be carried seaward and to extend the headland farther east. This still occurs to some degree, even though the dunes are now covered with trees. When the Commission acquired the land in 1922, it was already partially covered by heather (*Calluna vulgaris*) as well as marram grass, and formed a wild uninhabited heath where grouse—normally upland birds—nested. Afforestation with Scots and Corsican pine was successfully accomplished by 1945, working from the inland verge towards the east. Shelter was thus gradually provided against the prevailing south-west wind, for the sea-shore dunes, which alone remained mobile. The whole moor is now a thriving pine forest. Access has been provided for visitors to reach the remote sandy beaches. The eastern shoreline and the coastal dunes, which attract many species of gulls, shelduck, and eider duck to nest each spring, have been declared a Nature Reserve.

East Anglia

In East Anglia there is a noteworthy example of dune reclamation by private estate owners, the Coke family, famous in agriculture, on their Holkham estate near Blakeney in Norfolk. Between 1865 and 1890 these enterprising landowners planted a belt of pines, mainly Corsican, but with some Scots, maritime and Austrian pines, some five kilometres long, along the line of sand dunes that faces north to the North Sea. Their object was to provide shelter to the rich farmland lying inland, and to resist encroachment by the sea. It has been found that sand blown off the beach accumulates so effectively on the seaward face of the pine-clad dune

that the sea is, in effect, "pushed backwards". This is no doubt due to the
influence of the trees in reducing the lateral speed of offshore winds,
which are obliged to rise upwards to pass over the trees, or else filter
slowly through them. This stabilized dune held firm against the
tremendous tidal surge of 31st January 1953, though serious inundations
occurred elsewhere along the coast.

Lancashire

This shelterbelt development has a parallel at Formby in Lancashire, on
the coast of the Irish Sea between Southport and Liverpool. Here the
problem was to stabilize the vast quantities of sand that drifted inland
from the huge tidal sandbanks of the Mersey estuary before the prevailing
south-west wind. This was successfully achieved, from the mid-nineteenth
century onwards, by private estate owners who established a system of
shelterbelts of Corsican pine. This protected the inland farms and the
later housing developments. Some of the duneland nearer the sea has been
embodied in a Nature Reserve; other stretches have become golf links;
but some seven kilometres of irregular pinewoods survive, in a rough
crescent west of Formby.

Wales

In South Wales, on the coast of Carmarthenshire between Carmarthen
and Llanelly, a remarkable sandspit extends seawards, south-west of the
village of Pembrey. It seems to originate in sand carried downstream by
the River Towy, or eroded from the coast, and then carried eastwards by
sea currents. In 1928 the Forestry Commission acquired 1800 hectares
of these dunes, and their afforestation proceeded steadily on the lines
that had been pioneered at Culbin. Marram grass, artificially established,
was the main medium for sand stabilization, and Corsican pine was the
principal species used. Unfortunately, in the 1939–1945 war, this isolated
uninhabited spot attracted the attention of the Defence Departments,
and half the area was converted to other uses—an air field, firing ranges,
and an explosives factory.

The Commission's enterprise at Newborough, in the southern corner
of Anglesey, has been more fortunate. Here some 800 hectares of dunes
have been successfully planted, mainly with Corsican pine, since work
began in 1947.

Newborough Warren has an ancient history that matches that of Culbin.
It stands at the southern end of the Menai Straits that divide Anglesey
from the Welsh mainland; its original name, still preserved in local
Welsh speech, is Aber Menai—the mouth of the Menai Straits. By
tradition the Princes of Gwynedd, down to the thirteenth century,

anchored their navy in a spacious harbour there. After the English invasion under Edward I, castles were built at Caernarvon on the mainland facing Newborough, and also at Beaumaris on Anglesey. The inhabitants of a township called Llanfaes, close to Beaumaris, were resettled at Aber Menai, which was renamed, in English, as Newborough. Founded in 1303, it became the market town for a thriving agricultural area, a port, and a centre of local and overseas trade. It ranked as a royal manor and a seat of justice. The remains of buildings and field boundaries can still be found among the dunes, up to one kilometre seaward of the present limit of cultivable land.

But from the year 1331 onwards, sand drifting in from Cardigan Bay on the south, before the prevailing strong south-westerly winds, began to choke the harbour and threaten the town. Towards the end of the fifteenth century, navigation ended and trade ceased, and Newborough declined to a sleepy village, on the edge of a vast curving waste of sand, three kilometres deep with a shoreline seven kilometres long. Sheep, cattle and horses were pastured on its sparse grass, and rabbits were trapped, but its main value was as a source of marram grass which the local people made into mats, ropes, brooms, chairs, hassocks and cushions. During the 1939–1945 war the Warren was used for military training, which increased the damage to the turf already done by rabbits, and allowed the bare dunes to drift again.

The Forestry Commission is concerned with the western half of the sandhills, close to the rock promontory called Llanddwyn Island, which has now become joined to the Warren by a sandspit. The eastern half is a Nature Conservancy reserve. The Commission's first problem was to halt the inland movement of the dunes, so that trees could be planted free of the threat of inundation by sand. The method used, copied from a similar project on the Landes coastline of the Bay of Biscay in southwest France, was to build a simple brushwood fence along the irregular crest of the outermost dune on the seaward side—the *littoral dune*. Although this fence was no more than 1½ metres high, it had the effect of causing the wind to rise over it, and as it did so the sand it carried fell and began to bury the fence. After the fence has been thus reduced to about half its effective height, it is levered up, and the process of sand deposition continues. In this way the littoral dune was gradually raised, over a spell of six years, to a height of six metres. At the same time it became broader, spreading out on both inland and seaward sides, and it has had the effect of pushing back the powerful, menacing sea by creating a broad sloping beach that resists erosion, save in the fiercest of storms.

The sea was, in fact, forced so far back that in 1957 steps were taken to form a second littoral dune, some 25 m to seaward of the first. This too has proved successful and the sea is still in retreat. Both dunes have been effectively stabilized with marram grass, planted artificially. Thatching has been applied only in exceptionally difficult places, where blowouts have occurred. Newborough, on the edge of the Gulf Stream, has a warm climate and a low rainfall. Its summers are hot and sunny, even when clouds are forming massively over the Snowdonian mountains just to the east. It provides an ideal climate for Corsican pine, brought in from its Mediterranean isle.

Fortunately this tree is surprisingly resistant to sea salt. Researches by R. S. Edwards and Miss S. M. Claxton of the Department of Agriculture, University College of Wales, Aberystwyth, from 1961 to 1963, gave a measure of its rate of deposition. It averages 6·5 micrograms of sodium chloride per square centimetre per hour, but can rise to five times that figure when the winds blow strongly off the sea. When this occurs during dry spells, with no rain to wash the salt off tree foliage, it becomes concentrated by the sun's rays to the point where it causes leaf scorch. The needles of Corsican pine are often scorched brown on the seaward side of exposed trees, but the seaward foliage gives protection to all other foliage lying in its lee.

Other sites

The splendid sandy beach at Newborough naturally attracts many visitors, and access has been provided via a car park beside the forest.

Two other littoral areas tackled by the Commission merit brief mention. One is the Dunragit Sandhills, also called the Torrs Warren, in the west of Galloway, on its southern coast just west of New Luce in Wigtownshire. Here sand blown northwards from the broad beaches of Luce Bay has built up a narrow crescent-shaped dune system, which has been successfully afforested with Corsican pine, following marram planting and thatching.

The second scheme, which ended in failure, was on the Sands of Dunnet, east of Thurso in Caithness. Here a curving bay faces north-west, and is struck by frequent fierce gales that have piled up low mobile dunes. Corsican pine failed to thrive here because the sands proved too alkaline, having a high proportion of sea shells consisting of calcium carbonate. The site was transferred to the local council to make a recreational beach, but has since attracted the attention of oilmen who plan to build a giant rig on these sloping shores.

Inland dunes

A little known sandhill reclamation project was carried out by the

Forestry Commission in Lincolnshire, between 1930 and 1945, on the Laughton dunes to the east of the River Trent, between Gainsborough and Scunthorpe. The source of the sand was the great Trent itself, which here approaches sea-level and lacks the force to carry its burden farther. The prevailing south-west wind carried the sand eastwards, to form a heathery waste, some 800 hectares in extent. Scots and Corsican pines were successfully used to establish thriving pinewoods, and remove a threat to the very fertile farmland nearby.

Thetford Forest, around Thetford town on the borders of Norfolk and Suffolk, covers 21,000 hectares and is the largest in England. Practically all of this was formerly "breckland", a strange heathy wilderness on a substratum of pure sand that overlies a chalk bedrock. This sand is a relic of Tertiary deposits, much later in time than the chalk below, that were subject to glacial action during the Ice Age. At some time during the Middle Ages, some combination of unwise farming practices—possibly shifting cultivation, since "breckland" is Danish for "tilled land", or too intensive pasturage of sheep—destroyed the natural vegetation. The result is vividly described by John Evelyn, the famous Restoration diarist and forestry pioneer. He visited Thetford in 1667 and wrote:

The Travelling Sands, about 10 miles wide of Euston (an estate east of Thetford) that have so damaged the country, rouling from place to place, and like the Sands in the Deserts of Lybia, quite overwhelmed some gentlemen's whole estates.

The outcome was the impoverishment of large tracts of agricultural land, and its degradation to poor heathy pastures. During the eighteenth and nineteenth centuries, landowners strove to reclaim the brecks. One of their more effective measures was the planting of many miles of shelterbelts of Scots pine criss-crossing the wastes. But the soils still remained too poor for sustained agriculture, and from 1920 onwards many broad tracts of land were sold or leased to the Forestry Commission. Scots pine was the main species used in the first phase of afforestation, from 1920 to 1950. Since then, increasing use has been made of the higher-yielding Corsican pine.

The Thetford sand country extends north-westwards towards the town of Swaffham. It has a parallel in the Suffolk heath forest of Aldewood, which holds 3000 hectares of pinewoods between Woodbridge and Aldeburgh.

Although there has been no real sand fixation problem in these East Anglian forests during the Forestry Commission's era, the management is very conscious that it operates in a historically recent dune region. The sand, though seldom more than a few feet deep, is present everywhere, save in narrow river valleys. It sets the tone for sharp drainage, low fertility, and even the temperature regime, since it insulates the surface soil from the bedrock. Attempts to diversify the forest by bringing in trees other than the sand-, frost- and drought-tolerant pines, have met with little success; broad-leaved trees are checked by drought, lack of nutrients, and severe spring frosts.

The Thetford example shows that afforestation can only partially restore the value of good farmland smothered by sand dunes. It can halt dune spread, as it has probably done at Culbin, but cannot re-create the old fertility which lies buried below. Sand remains a persistent sterilant, even though it is a manageable substratum for an economic timber crop.

FURTHER READING

Bain, George (1922), *The Culbin Sands or The Story of a Buried Estate*, Nairnshire Telegraph, Nairn.

Edlin, Herbert L. (1951), *British Plants and their Uses*, Batsford, London.

Forestry Commission (1950), *Britain's Forests: Culbin*, Her Majesty's Stationery Office, London.

Holtam, B. W. (1971), *Windblow of Scottish Forests in January 1968*, Forestry Commission Bulletin 45, Her Majesty's Stationery Office, Edinburgh.

Mackie, W. (1899), "The Sands and Sandstones of Eastern Moray", *Transactions of the Edinburgh Geological Society*, **7**, p. 148.

Ovington, J. D. (1950). "The Afforestation of the Culbin Sands", *Journal of Ecology*, **38**, pp. 303–319.

Salisbury, E. (1952), *Downs and Dunes*, Bell, London.

Senex, I. (1721), *A New Map of Scotland according to Gordon of Straloch, Revised and Improved*. A reprint of an earlier seventeenth-century Gordon map that antedates the Culbin storm of 1694.

Steers, J. A. (1953), *The Sea Coast*, Collins, London.

CHAPTER TWO

OPENCAST MINING AND THE ENVIRONMENT

D. J. HARLEY

Surface mining

"Surface mining"—these words can cause a lover of the environment to bristle with indignation as he pictures devastation, with the earth's surface upturned and devoid of life. Why should there be this reaction? It is because the post-war escalation of surface mining outside the United Kingdom has focused attention on the strange way in which we use our natural resources.

Man uses land to achieve the greatest personal profit, and each generation tends to have only temporary interest in the land. Our descendants inherit what we leave. We can be selfish in not caring how we use the land, or we can plan to be unwasteful with what we inherited and are passing to the next generation.

Wholesale felling of trees without re-afforestation, or subsequent control of storm water to prevent soil erosion on the bare slopes, may make paper a cheaper commodity today. Concentrated grazing by cattle, without resting or fertilizing the grass land, may provide cheaper meat whilst there is plenty of grass. The longer-term result, however, may be the creation of waste areas. Surface mining on a vast scale, conducted without thought for consequential effect, has become a matter of concern in some parts of the world, and has produced opposition which could bring the operation to a halt. This is illogical; there has to be a planned compromise so that needs, as far as possible, are met.

In the war and post-war years, wealth and power have rested more heavily on the exploitation and use of mineral resources. Output and time are the parents of wealth. The higher the degree of mechanization, the more quickly and cheaply can minerals be produced. Surface mining was an ideal subject for exploitation. One man with a spade might excavate 2 to 2·5 cubic metres (m^3) of medium-hard soil in a day. An excavating machine with a bucket capable of taking $110 m^3$ in each bite could dig $38,200 m^3$ in the same 8-hour day. Machines can be scaled up to match the size of the task and, for instance, in the coalfields of the United States, a dragline of $165 m^3$ bucket capacity is in use. Unfortunately, in some operations there was no allocation of time (and therefore of profit) in preparation for, and execution of, land reclamation in the wake of mineral extraction. This situation is, however, being improved rapidly. In the period 1930 to 1971, the United States mining industry (surface and underground) used 3·65 million acres—less than 0·20% of the area of the country —of which 1·46 million acres were reclaimed. Therefore 2·19 million acres were left waste—a small percentage maybe, but still a lot of land. In 1971, 80% of land used in that year for the industry was reclaimed; most of this was done by companies engaged in surface mining for bituminous coal. The term *reclamation* in these statistics means reconditioning or restoring in compliance with the law; where no reclamation is required by law, the operating companies have made their own estimates of land returned to a useful condition.

The need for vigilance is apparent in many other parts of the world as society demands more coal, copper, phosphate rock, uranium, clays, and aggregates. But society also wants these minerals as cheaply as possible, and it is hard to accept the fact that we should pay more so that land can be restored in another country. We must all share responsibility for what has happened, since we have all taken some benefit from the rape of the land.

Restoration to original use is not always possible; restoration to alternative use may not be feasible; reclamation beyond a general tidying-up may not be practical. The possibilities are restricted by terrain, climate, the type of mineral deposit and the method of mining. It is essential that if open-cast mining (an economical way of obtaining much-needed minerals) is to be conditioned by restoration or reclamation restrictions, these must be reasonably achievable.

However, there is more to man's environment than the view he gets from his house or from his car. Noise, dust, water pollution and human safety can be affected by surface mining. Whose environmental problem is the greatest? The safety of a banksman supervising the reversing of large trucks to the edge of a tipping point is better protected if the vehicles automatically sound a klaxon horn as they reverse; he is then warned that a truck driver is operating without full vision. For the banksman, the klaxon makes a safer working environment; but a lady living half a mile away may be annoyed by the sound of a horn occurring every few minutes.

Legislation and Codes of Practice to protect the environment have been, and are being introduced into the United Kingdom. These arise from general consultations, and have not been rushed into law, thereby imposing impractical restrictions on individual operations. Indeed many surface-mining companies in the United Kingdom excavating sand and gravel, clay and iron ore have voluntarily adopted measures to preserve the environment. Some imaginative reclamation or restoration projects have been designed and executed.

The record of social responsibility in the National Coal Board's opencast mining in Great Britain is particularly good. Before looking at the reasons why the Board's Opencast Executive is now able to put forward mining proposals normally acceptable to planning authorities and other affected interests, the reader should have an understanding of the various methods of surface mining.

Methods of surface mining

In simple terms, surface mining means the removal of all soils, glacial drift, shales and rock overlying the deposit which is to be won. What are the advantages of such operations, compared with underground working from a shaft or adit?

(1) The mineral extraction can in some cases be 100% of the deposit.
(2) Minerals can be won where ground or geological conditions prohibit underground methods.
(3) Surface mining generally has a lower cost per unit of production because of high mechanization.
(4) The extent of the operation can be more easily tailored to suit the economics of working.

The market value of a given quantity of mineral limits the quantity of non-revenue-producing waste which can be excavated to obtain the mineral. This economic ratio between overburden and mineral is affected by the type of overburden, ground location, climate, the capacity of available excavating plant, and many other considerations which affect mining costs, such as environmental protection and reclamation requirements. The main methods of surface mining are:

(1) open pit
(2) opencast or strip
(3) auger
(4) hydraulic
(5) dredging.

Open pit
Open pit is a quarrying operation. The ratio of overburden to mineral is usually low. The deposit being worked provides a large quantity of

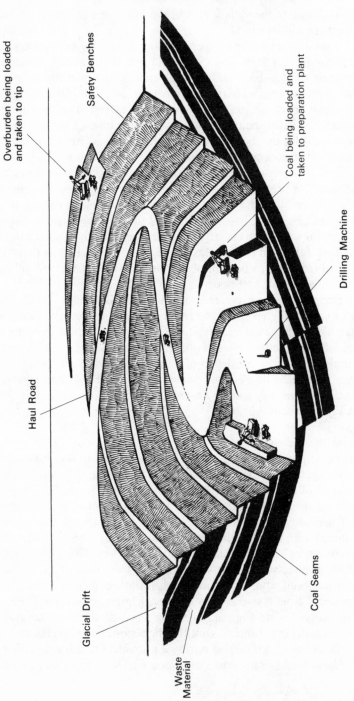

Overburden being loaded and taken to tip

Safety Benches

Coal being loaded and taken to preparation plant

Drilling Machine

Haul Road

Glacial Drift

Waste Material

Coal Seams

Figure 2.1 Open-pit mining.

mineral in relation to the surface area of the mine, and at the end of the operation there will be a void.

Rock or slate quarries are in open pits, but frequently entail working into a hillside from a level base. Sand and gravel extracting is mainly from relatively shallow beds, and the problems are not as great as in the deeper open pits associated with mining copper, coal and iron ore.

In the normal deep operation, the mineral is extracted on a series of levels connecting with a haulage road down to the base of the pit (figure 2.1). The vertical distance between the extracting levels is often conditioned by the reach of the excavating machinery being used. Such workings may use face shovels which utilize the power and weight of the excavator to break out solid (or pre-blasted) material with a forward lifting movement of a bucket. When filled, the bucket is traversed to discharge its load into a waiting truck. The truck hauls the material to a loading or preparation point if mineral is being won, or to a discharge point in a worked-out part of the pit if the load is mine waste. The mine is designed so that the haulage road from top to bottom of the pit is at a gradient best suited to the performance of the trucks.

This description of one typical open-pit method should enable the reader to visualize the void, with terraced sides remaining, when such a mine has yielded a large volume of mineral which has left the area forever. There are, of course, other styles of operating, using different equipment. For example, excavators consisting of a machine driving a wheel, fitted with series of digging buckets, are sometimes used. These buckets discharge their loads as they start to descend, and the material may then be carried away on a conveyor belt.

Opencast or strip mining
Opencast or strip mining is a system of digging similar to that we might adopt in a vegetable garden. First a trench is excavated down to the deposit, either following it down the dip of the mineral or parallel with its outcrop. If taken down-dip, the first trench, or *box cut* as it is usually called, will probably extend from the shallowest to the deepest part of the mine. Material from the box cut is dumped in mounds along the nearest edge of ground which is not to be excavated. The deposit is then extracted and removed, probably by a relatively small face shovel and truck. When the deposit has been won, a second trench is cut parallel with the first and the material from it is cast into the trench previously made (figure 2.2). The process of removing the mineral is repeated. This operation is carried on in a series of parallel cuts until all the deposit has been taken out.

Ideally the excavation is carried out by a dragline. On this excavating machine, a large bucket is fitted to a wire rope, which in turn is suspended

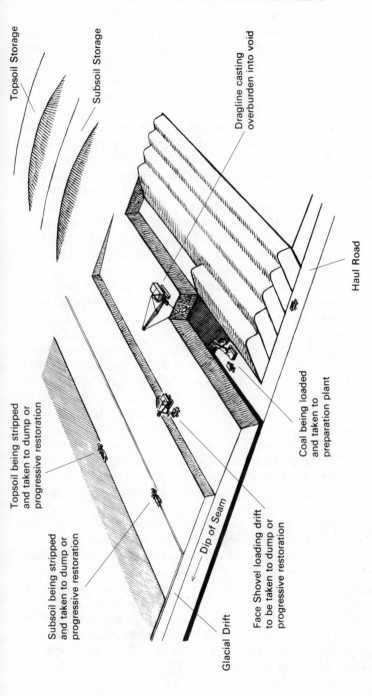

Topsoil Storage

Subsoil Storage

Dragline casting overburden into void

Haul Road

Topsoil being stripped and taken to dump or progressive restoration

Subsoil being stripped and taken to dump or progressive restoration

Coal being loaded and taken to preparation plant

Dip of Seam

Glacial Drift

Face Shovel loading drift to be taken to dump or progressive restoration

Figure 2.2 Opencast mining.

from a long boom. The bucket is swung and dropped to the digging face, and then drawn back towards the machine. Teeth on the leading edge of the bucket bite into the overburden, which must be fragmented or reasonably soft, and the bucket fills as it is raised. The machine then traverses, swings the bucket outwards, and tips it so that the material is cast to form a heap. As the machine moves along to excavate a trench, the cast spoil forms a ridge with a series of peaks.

Main excavation by dragline is the cheapest method, because the material is cut and deposited in its final position without subsequent handling by ancillary mechanical plant. For this reason, the recent tendency in the United States has been to concentrate on increasing the size and power of draglines rather than of shovels. To produce the most economical excavation, the machine must be capable of reaching the lowest point of the workings, and of casting well into the previous trench. This may entail building an excavator of huge proportions, and is worth while only where it will have a full operational life on one mine. Smaller excavating plant may have a power unit mounted on crawlers which can be fitted with front-end shovel equipment or a drag bucket on a longer boom. Large machines are specially designed with power/weight ratio suited to one use. They are usually mounted, not on crawl tracks, but on a circular base to give low ground pressure. To move the excavator forwards or backwards the weight is taken on eccentrically mounted pads on either side. The machine lifts and drags itself a few feet at a time in the required direction; the pads then reposition themselves for the next movement. More generally in Britain the opencast mine has to be worked by a combination of motor scraper, or shovel and truck, from the surface down to a level from which the dragline can operate to the pit bottom. This puts the trucks on to the more economic haul, with less height to climb than if working from the lower section of the cut, and provides the ability to transport and tip upper measures where required, possibly in dumps for future use. The dragline would then stand on the excavated level and be able to cast directly into the worked out cut.

The final result, if there is no attempt at reclamation, will be a high ridge of cast overburden standing on original ground, and a series of parallel peaked ridges where cuts have been backfilled. There will be an open trench at the terminal side of the mine.

Opencast mining for oil-bearing shales has a special problem; the eventual debris occupies more space than the excavated material. Such shales were mined in the Lothians in Scotland by underground methods, and it remains to be seen whether their value will ever increase sufficiently to make opencasting a worthwhile proposition. The excavated shale has to be heated to around 900 °F, when organic matter vaporizes and is condensed to a crude oil. The remaining burnt shale has then increased in volume. If a large-scale project is envisaged, great quantities of water are necessary for the preparation process, and there must be provision for disposal or spreading the extra material.

Contour mining

Contour mining, which is a type of opencast mining, consists of following a mineral outcrop along a hillside and working into the hill, as far as is economic, in a series of cuts parallel with the first from which the spoil has probably been deposited down the lower hillside. On completion of the operation, there will remain a level strip or bench along the side slope of the hill. The inside of the bench will be a bared face of solid strata, and the outside will be heaped waste or, more likely, the rim of the hill. If uncontrolled, the tipped waste may cause landslides, blockage of rivers and drainage channels, erosion and water pollution.

Where a thick regular deposit is apparent in the final high wall of an opencast mine, particularly if worked on a contour, it is not uncommon in some parts of the world for large augers to bore into the remaining mineral, which is removed like wood being cut by a carpenter's drill and bit.

Hydraulic mining

Hydraulic mining uses very powerful water jets against the side of an open pit or bank to wash down the waste material or the mineral being won. The slurry flows to a lagoon from which it is pumped, as required, to a preparation plant where the desired material is extracted. The waste or tailings lie in lagoons where the solids are allowed to settle. Surface water, which may still contain some suspended solids, is drained off and discharged into streams and rivers. If there is plenty of space, once filled lagoons may be abandoned; but if the settling areas have to be re-used, the solids are dug out and cast into heaps.

Dredging

Dredging is the excavation of material from the bottom of a flooded area, river or lake. It is carried out by equipment floating on a large raft. Specialized machinery, such as buckets on endless chains, or cutters and suction pumps, may be employed. Sometimes a dragline, with a clam shell bucket which operates with a grabbing action, is used from a raft. During working, there will probably be water pollution from the increased volume of suspended particles, but this is controllable where the water can be impounded for sufficient time to allow settlement of solids. The final result is to leave a stretch of water deeper than previously existed.

Opencast coal mining in the United Kingdom

There are fundamental differences between opencast coal mining in the United Kingdom and in the United States. In the early days, the Americans came to advise on how to plan and operate a mine; now they come to see what can be achieved to protect amenities and provide final land restoration, and how such environmental considerations can be adapted to their own needs.

Opencast mining for coal, using hand labour, has been going on for nearly 2000 years. During the last war the increased demand for fuel placed a heavy demand on traditional deep mining from collieries, and the Government decided to augment coal supplies by increasing opencast work.

So we had a Government-controlled activity operated by private enterprise. The Ministry decided when and from where the coal should be won, and did so in consultation with other Ministries, such as Agriculture, whose interests would be affected. Civil-engineering companies with experience in excavation provided the limited know-how, machinery and men, and worked under contract to the Government. The profit motive was held in check as far as was practicable by a contract which required the safeguarding of other interests.

Three considerations favour opencast mining in Britain:

(a) Shallow coal deposits in Britain are relatively thin and limited in areas. The size of opencast sites is thereby restricted, and the volume of mineral removed is normally low in relation to overburden disturbed. This enables restoration to near original levels.

(b) We normally have soil, peat, or soil-making material to use as a restored surface layer.

(c) Our temperate climate, whilst making excavation wet and difficult, gives enough sun and rain to promote growth of vegetation on restored areas.

From 1941 until 1958 opencast mining was not controlled by normal planning legislation but operated under the Defence (General) Regulations 1939, with the Ministry of Works taking responsibility. Although the Ministry could have been ruthless or thoughtless in the use of its powers, it was always the practice that local authorities, statutory undertakings, and persons having an interest in the land, were consulted before any site was mined. In areas where there existed an over-riding agricultural value, also of great importance in time of war, no site was worked. From the start of the Government's involvement in opencasting for coal, it was decided that the working area should be restored to original use. Expertise was not available to ensure that the best restoration results were obtained, but the decision to restore land was an enlightened one, and the Ministry (Department in Scotland) of Agriculture took a keen interest in achieving success. Pride in producing better results became as important as pride in producing the maximum tonnage of coal from each site. All engaged in the operation sought to gain by experience. This attitude generated an impetus which has never been lost. To the contractor, a good restoration meant the likelihood of more opencast contracts. To the Authority it meant easier consultation for successive sites.

Compensation to land owners and occupiers was paid under the Compensation (Defence) Act 1939, and was determined in a fair manner. It can be seen that Government involvement in opencast coal mining ensured that a decision to commence work rested with a Minister, not a private individual, and in a democratic way that Minister considered other interests which might be temporarily harmed. In authorizing the operation, the Minister laid down, for each site, a list of conditions to be observed during occupation of the requisitioned land. Over the years, control was passed from the Ministry of Works to the Ministry of Fuel and Power (later the Ministry of Fuel).

Use of Defence Regulations to acquire rights in land for opencast mining purposes was acceptable during wartime conditions and immediately afterwards. When it became apparent that a nucleus of sites would have to continue coal production, it also became apparent that land requisitioning by use of Defence Regulations was not in keeping with peacetime political thought. Opencast production was making a useful contribution to coal supplies, and was being viewed by many countries as the economic mining method to be exploited. But in the United Kingdom it was not for many years felt to be of sufficiently lasting importance to warrant special legislation to take over from the Governmental wartime compulsory powers.

In 1947 coal mining in the United Kingdom became the responsibility of the National Coal Board, which had been formed under the Coal Industry Nationalization Act. Opencast mining was not brought into the orbit of the Board until 1952, and for a further six years continued to operate under the defence legislation.

The year 1958 saw the introduction of the Opencast Coal Act, a rather cumbersome piece of planning legislation which laid down the procedure under which the National Coal Board had to obtain a Government Minister's authorization for each opencast side it wished to work; the Act gave the bases on which compensation was to be assessed. Although the majority of coal reserves in the United Kingdom are vested in the National Coal Board, other minerals associated with coal seams, such as brickearth, fireclay and ironstone, only came into the Board's ownership if they belonged to the old coal companies whose assets had passed into public possession. Some such minerals may now be owned by persons with no other interest in the land. The Act therefore had to provide for surface owners, mineral owners, land occupiers and agricultural tenants. Even where the National Coal Board owns the surface, coal, and other minerals, it still requires an authorization before working may commence.

From 1958 until 1970 opencast coal production was low. This was in line with the world-wide run down in demand for coal. Since the policy of the National Coal Board is that opencast mining, however profitable, must not displace deep-mined production, surface mining reached its lowest output of 6·2 million tons in 1969.

The National Coal Board had formed the Opencast Executive to deal with all activities under the Opencast Coal Act, and it is perhaps surprising that during the period of reduced activity the Board spent a great deal of thought on ways to make its operations more readily acceptable to planning and local authorities, and to the general public. One example of this is that during the late 1960s the Executive established nurseries where thousands of trees are grown for use on future opencast sites. They are used to assist in visual screening and to improve the appearance of some restorations. The trees are branch and root-pruned to give a well-shaped specimen with a strong compact root ball, making transplanting easier and more successful.

The basic factor of which all had to be made aware is that opencast mining is a transitory use of land in the same way as forestry or agriculture. We now have agriculture where once there were forests. We have forests planted by the Forestry Commission where there had previously been poor hill grazing. Whilst it would therefore seem economically sensible to excavate land in order to recover a quantity of coal far more valuable than many years' agricultural proceeds, it makes even more sense if that land could be restored to agriculture within a reasonable period.

At present the Department of Energy is responsible for authorizations made under the Opencast Coal Act. These are not granted as a matter of course, but require a balanced case to be presented for the Minister's consideration.

Prospecting
The first requirement is for the Board to know its reserves of shallow coal, the qualities of fuel available, and the physical problems of excavating. In this connection it is not always realized that coal seams vary in analysis, and those suitable for one industrial purpose are quite unacceptable for another. In addition to calorific value, we need to know the percentage content of ash, sulphur, volatile matter and moisture.

By studying the Ordnance Survey Geological Maps (scale 6″ to 1 mile) and abandoned mine records and plans, geologists on the staff of Opencast Executive identify areas where shallow coal may be found; they also gain some knowledge of the quality which might be expected. Having fixed an area to be prospected, the Board serves on the planning authority a notice of its intention to prospect. Copies of the notice, made as a direction order under regulations related to the Town and Country Planning Acts, are also sent to the Department of Energy and all statutory bodies such as those dealing with foresty, electricity transmission and distribution, telephones, water distribution, river purification, gas distribution, sewage disposal, roads, and the Nature Conservancy. The Department of Energy passes information on the proposals to the Departments of Environment, Agriculture and, in Scotland, to the Scottish Development Department which has responsibility for strategic planning. Agreement is reached with owners and occupiers to allow commencement of drilling operations. Following the notice of intention to prospect, six weeks are allowed before work actually starts. During this period, the observations of the various interests are carefully noted; where a statutory authority indicates it owns apparatus over or under the land this is located and recorded on a master plan.

The Opencast Executive, therefore, at a very early stage is aware of the complications, large or small, which will require consideration should it be decided, eventually, that there is sufficient coal available within the land to make it an economic proposition to mine. Prospecting is a thorough operation; some holes are drilled open and others cored. From the latter are taken coal seam analyses, and cores are stored so that the hardness of overlying rock can be gauged. It is essential to build up a comprehensive picture of the geological structure, and to establish the factors which will bear on the cost of excavating the coal.

The pattern of boreholes depends on the geological complexity of the area. If the coal is undisturbed and of consistent thickness, holes can be drilled on a grid system once the outcrop has been established. The hole pattern has to be irregular to record sufficient information where there are geological disturbances such as faults, anticlines, synclines and glacial washouts, or where the coal varies in thickness or quality. Every effort is made to reduce inconvenience to land occupiers, and to avoid interference with farming operations. Drilling is often organized, for instance, so that the rigs move on to land after a crop has been harvested, and prospecting continues until preparations are being made for sowing the next cereal or root crop. Similarly, drilling rigs are withdrawn from hill grazing at lambing time. Consideration of farming interests in this way complicates the geologists' work and increases cost, but it is part of the policy to minimize environmental disruption on any opencast activity. By Section 39 of the Opencast Coal Act 1958, the Board may request the appropriate Government Minister to issue a direction order which would give a right of entry for prospecting, but this action has seldom been taken.

Skeleton drilling will show that a site has potential. This is considered in relation to the external interests previously recorded. It is possible at that stage to decide whether to drill the site fully, or if the prospecting resources would be better employed elsewhere.

A fully-proved site will have a file of information covering borehole logs, typical vertical and horizontal geological sections, ground water levels, observations on strata and ground stability around the proposed excavation area, the maximum profitable tonnage of coal to be extracted, and the total volume and nature of the overburden to be handled. The analysis of the coal is estimated, enabling the type of market and saleable value to be assessed. The accuracy of this information is of importance, because all sites are worked on contracts between the Board and civil-engineering companies. The Board's anticipated profit on opencast coal sales could be adversely affected if the contractor had grounds for claiming losses as a result of misleading or insufficient information in tender documents. In the disturbed geological conditions general in Scotland, a site normally consists of a number of areas separated by faulting and surface features. A working site may eventually consist of parts of a number of prospecting sites, for it is rare for a site to consist of one large body of coal.

The files on fully-proved sites provide a bank of reserves from which can be drawn those required by the Board's marketing department to satisfy an anticipated demand which cannot be met by planned deep-mined output.

Bringing an opencast site into production
When estimates of output from collieries have been made and matched with estimated marketing requirements for electricity power stations, industrial users, coking and anthracitic fuel, there will most probably be a production gap. This is particularly applicable to the current situation, in which an increase in world-wide demand for coal, as an alternative to oil, has outstripped the ability to raise output by developing existing or new collieries. Opencast mining can provide the additional tonnage, and a site is normally in production within two months of commencement of work which may, however, be delayed by months or years by the need for consultation and negotiation.

When it has been decided that a site should be worked, the Executive's civil-engineering staff make preliminary estimates of the cost of excavating coal to different depths and from varying areas. The environmental and economic effect of excavating to the alternative schemes is then studied. With the site boundary provisionally delineated, the services of the District Valuer are obtained to negotiate purchase or lease of the land on behalf of the Board. Usually it is preferable for the Board to own the land, because this permits flexibility of restoration. If the occupier is a tenant who does not wish to have his interest bought out, the Board takes a sub-lease, paying rent and compensation for disturbance and loss of profits.

Whilst the land negotiations are proceeding, an informal approach is made to those authorities or statutory bodies who would be affected by opencast mining. The Board's proposals for working (including measures for protection of amenity) are outlined, and comment or discussion invited. The object is to present information which it is hoped will enable the local authority to accept the project. Sometimes compromise has to be reached on certain sections of the planning, but always a viable mining operation must be retained.

An application is finally made by the Board to the Secretary of State, seeking authorization of the site in terms of the Opencast Coal Act. The application is accompanied by a formal document consisting of three schedules which, together with a plan and a Statement of Case, present complete information on which the Minister can base his decision. The First Schedule consists of a detailed description of the location of the land, its owners, occupiers and lessees, and of its present use. Rights of way, buildings, watercourses, tree preservation orders, historical ruins, areas of special scientific interest, and apparatus owned by statutory authorities are all described.

The Second Schedule explains the working proposals, the depths of top soil and sub-soil likely to be recovered and stored, the amount of coal to be won and the minimum, maximum and average depth of dig. It tells whether the various interests described in the First Schedule will be preserved or, if not preserved, how they will be dealt with. It also states the measures to be taken to preserve local amenities. The Third Schedule explains to what after-use the land is to be put, and how it will be restored for that purpose. The Board is required to give notice of intention to apply for an authorization by publishing formal statements in both local press and the London or Edinburgh Gazette. A period of 28 days is given during which local authorities or persons with a direct interest in the land may raise objections. The Board is given the opportunity to try to resolve any objections, but if it fails, a Public Inquiry is arranged. Here the objectors and the Board state their cases before an Inspector appointed by the Department of the Environment. The Inspector makes a report to the Secretary of State for Energy, following which a decision is made to authorize the site or to refuse that particular application. The Board may re-apply for a site, with or without modifications, whenever it feels a change of circumstances warrants a new submission.

If it is necessary to deny public access over a right of way during the working of a site, an application for the temporary suspension or stopping-up of the path or road is made. Where practicable, alternative ways are provided, but in any case the order will require the Board to reinstate the right of way on its original route, unless the local or highway authority obtain a separate order for its variation.

Working a site

Whilst the Minister's decision is awaited, the Opencast Executive's civil engineers will be marshalling the promises and agreements made during the planning negotiations, and interpreting the measures as clauses in a contractual specification. A safe working method is devised, and the theoretical mechanical plant and labour requirements established. An estimated cost is made of all works, including amenity protection and physical restoration. An authorization contains conditions of working normally based on the measures offered by the Board in its application to the Minister. These conditions are studied to ensure the draft site contract will put them into effect. Selected civil-engineering companies are then invited to submit tendered prices for carrying out the contract. The companies must also give statements and plans showing the proposed method of working, which will be appraised without reference to financial comparisons, to ensure that the Executive is satisfied as to the safety of the mining method. A contract will be let to the company offering the best price and method. The Opencast Executive then nominates staff to be responsible for supervising the operation of the contract.

The safety aspect is assuming increased importance because, as the value of coal rises, it becomes economic to excavate deeper at a higher ratio of overburden to coal. Whereas in the immediate post-war period bituminous coal for power stations would be mined at a ratio of up to 8 to 1, now 16 to 1 can be sensible, and for particularly valuable anthracitic coals a ratio of more than 25 to 1 may be used. These ratios are taken on an excavation vertically sided, measured in the solid. In assessing the actual volume of overburden to be moved, we have to bear in mind the material in the sloping sides of the excavation, the safety benches to be made at intervals to prevent slipped overburden from falling to the bottom of the cut, and the bulking factor or percentage by which each cubic metre of solid will increase in volume when broken and lifted.

Sites are normally worked by opencast methods, the main exception being the open pit at Westfield in Fife, from which more than 12 million tons of coal have been extracted with a further 11 million tons yet to be won. (In that instance the coal lies in a basin, rather than in outcrop strips and, since such a large quantity of mineral is saleable, it is inevitable there will be a hole left at the end of operations.) With very few exceptions, therefore, partial restoration is progressive as the cuts move across the coal area. The ability to complete restoration for agricultural or afforestation purposes lies in conservation of soils, sub-soil, and soil-making material.

Conservation of soils

The first task of the contractor is to strip all available top soil from land over which plant will run during the opening-up process, and to extend the stripping over a coal-bearing area sufficiently large to give several months of overburden excavation. Top soil is usually lifted by motor scrapers operating on a circuit. These machines are capable of removing soil to fine limits so that none is wasted, but they have to be used under fairly dry conditions to achieve these results. Since stripping is carried out by several scrapers moving at high speed on ground level, this is inevitably a noisy process, although of short duration. The soil is carried to special dumps from which it will not be moved until required for restoration. These dumps are usually constructed at strategic points along the site boundary, so that they act as sound baffles and, when seeded with grass, they soften the visual disturbance of mining. If the level of surrounding land is similar to (or lower than) the site levels, then green top-soil mounds may screen the operation entirely, and indeed trees and shrubs are often planted as a method of breaking the somewhat rigid outline of mounds.

Coal measures are usually found in association with mudstone, shales and clays; these are materials which tend to form hard surfaces when traversed by machinery engaged on restoration. It is important to provide, where possible, an alternative layer of material between the restored soil and the overburden. Where there is a sub-soil, it is the practice to strip this and store separately, in the same manner as top soil. In addition, during overburden excavation, watch is kept for soil-making material, usually soft sandstone which breaks down in dump. The aim is to get sufficient sub-soil and other suitable material to provide a layer 0·60 metre deep over the restored site. For every hectare of land excavated or used for roads, buildings, etc., there are about 3000 m³ of soil and 6000 m³ of sub-soil to be stacked away from the mounds of overburden which will be formed later. Whereas the local planner wishes to have the site area as small as possible, to minimize the impact on agriculture and local interests, it is in the interests of operation, protection of amenities and restoration that there must be ample room for activities which, although not essential to opencast mining, are part of the Board's working policy.

In moorland and poorly drained areas, such as those used for seasonal grazing by sheep, there may be only a few inches of soil in places, with peat overlying much of the ground. Peat varies considerably in type and is frequently difficult to handle. If it is sufficiently fibrous in nature, it can be excavated by a dragline standing on solid ground. This peat can be mixed in mound with sandy materials or sub-soils, and used to provide a surface layer for restoration to grass or forestry. Alternatively peat can be held in pre-formed bunds, for subsequent use. Peat which becomes very liquid when disturbed is best discarded, to a pre-determined safe depth, in a void where it can be contained whilst overburden is tipped into it until the mass becomes stable.

Minimizing disturbance

Throughout the life of a working site, steps are taken to reduce to a practical minimum any adverse effect on local environment. Noise can often be reduced by use of baffle mounds as previously described, but it may be useless to deflect noise where houses are on a higher level than a nearby opencast working, or when machinery is being used well above ground level, as during construction of a long-term overburden dump.

The Board therefore requires all machines and vehicles to be properly silenced, and indeed brings pressure to bear on manufacturers if their standard equipment is not quiet enough in use. In addition, all vehicles, excavators, and plant are fitted with suppressors to prevent interference with television or radio reception in the neighbourhood.

Working hours may be restricted in certain districts if the site is close to houses. This restriction may apply to the entire operation or to plant working above original ground level, because an excavator digging well down in a cut is scarcely audible under many conditions. Of course it has to be remembered that limitation of working hours prolongs the active life of an opencast site, and this may be undesirable.

It is inevitable that dust will be created by the handling of overburden and the movement of plant over stripped areas. An opencast contract requires every means, including watering, of suppressing dust in order to prevent nuisance to neighbouring properties. Water bowsers constructed on motor scrapers have been found to be very effective, since these machines can climb onto dumps, or run down into cuts and lay dust.

Blasting is carried out, but not to bring down rock from a face as in normal quarrying. The object is to break hard strata to facilitate digging by a machine. Blasting restrictions are laid down, limiting the maximum weight of explosive to an amount calculated after site tests by independent recognized experts. The charge may be further reduced to comply with the Board's limits of amplitude of vibration, namely 0·1 mm at any building or public service, and 0·06 mm at any occupied dwelling. The permitted hours of blasting are also restricted, so that local residents become accustomed to the sound occurring at certain times rather as an inhabitant of Edinburgh may seldom notice the one-o'clock gun fired from the Castle.

In common with other trades and industries, the Board requires from the appropriate River Board a consent to discharge water from an opencast site, even though the point of discharge is in an existing water course. The consent lays down conditions which state the upper and lower limits of pH value, the maximum proportion of suspended solids, and requires that there be no visible trace of oil or grease. Settling lagoons and traps are constructed so that the conditions can be met, unless extraordinary weather causes temporary but insuperable difficulties.

Access to the mine will be only at points previously agreed with the local authority; vehicles leaving must be clean, so as not to deposit mud or slurry on public roads, and lorries which are carrying coal from the site, or returning empty to it, are usually required to use a road route accepted by the local or highway authority.

Safety

Since opencasting is usually carried out in areas where there has been underground mining for shallow coal in years past, it is not uncommon to excavate into shafts or adits whose existence had not been recorded in old plans. These are made safe by filling and capping under technical direction, and provide a land improvement which would not otherwise have occurred.

The working environment of those employed in the mining operation is conditioned by the law relating to safety and health in mines and quarries. As an additional measure, geologists or civil engineers with specialist knowledge are employed to advise on slope safety and on the stability of ground upon which large overburden mounds may be or have been built. Advice of such nature can be a protection against damage to neighbouring land or property, as well as assisting the operation of a safe opencast site.

Restoration

On completion of excavation, overburden previously dumped is returned to the excavation area, which is then levelled and regraded. The contours may be similar to the original but, if there had been low-lying land, the ground form may be altered. The aim is to make an area which is self-draining, but this may not be possible if surrounding land is higher. It may be best to grade the restoration so that it drains to one low area deliberately established in a convenient location. Freedom to alter contours depends, as with other restoration factors, on the land ownership. The proprietor's wishes must be respected if they are practical.

The bulking of overburden through excavation is reduced after the material has been given time to settle and, depending on the type of strata disturbed, the residual bulking will probably be in the order of 8%. On the earlier sites, where the economic limit of extraction of overburden to bituminous coal was about 8:1, there was roughly a 3% loss in volume of material, thus giving a slight lowering of restored levels in relation to the original. The value of coal has now risen and, providing the cost of opencast mining rises at a slower rate, the economic dig ratio will increase. Sites will be restored with a raising of levels rather than a lowering.

Several factors unite to determine the period before final settlement has taken place. The type of overburden, the method of back-filling, and the time taken for ground water levels to be established in the fill are vital points which can make a difference of years in the settlement time. Of course, where the restored land is required for a specific purpose such as road construction, the back-fill can be layered and consolidated at the time; but this is an expensive process, and is neither necessary nor desirable in agricultural land. Test levelling every six months for the first few years after restoration has shown that, on a normal site, the ground will have become stable in 3 to 5 years.

Should the land be required for forestry planting, the hill-and-dale effect of opencast mining by dragline may not be levelled off. Instead the hills are sometimes flattened so that the tops are about 4 metres wide. The sides are graded to a slope of 45° and the dales are filled to give a flat width of 5 to 6 metres. Under certain conditions this assists drainage, and permits the tops and slopes to be planted whilst the valleys are used for movement of materials and foresters. However, there are not always advantages from such restoration, and in many cases a normal re-contouring is preferable. Roads constructed for mining in hill areas can be of great use for future forestry purposes, and are left in good order instead of being removed on completion of coal winning.

The ground is then thoroughly rooted to remove any large boulders. In Scotland the practice is to double-root, the second run being parallel with or at right angles to the first. Large stones brought to the surface are then removed.

Rooting is carried out usually by a tracked machine to the rear of which are fitted tines about 0·80 metre in length and 1·0 metre apart. Pressure is applied to the tines by hydraulic equipment on the tractor.

Replacement of soils

The Ministry (or Department) of Agriculture are the Board's agents and advisers when restoration is to be to agriculture. Over the years, experience has been gained on a wide-ranging series of sites, so that good restoration results are now achieved. Rooting overburden breaks the hard-pan of clays crushed by the motor scrapers engaged on levelling, and permits penetration of surface water. Sub-soil or soil-making material is then spread on the overburden, to a depth of 0·60 metre if available; should the restoration be on a hillside, the motor scrapers discharge and spread whilst travelling along the slope. This reduces erosion by arresting the flow of surface water. Erosion is a significant problem on steep gradients. A series of small water flows at the high points gather momentum and unite into larger streams as they progress downhill. Ravines are formed on the lower reaches, as not only soil but loose overburden is carried on to flatter land. In these circumstances rooting will be parallel with the slope. The effect of rooting and soil spreading in this way is that machine tracks form water channels along the contours.

Soils stored in dumps tend to become acidic, and it is often the practice to apply lime at 3 tons per acre (7 tonnes per hectare) over the spread sub-soil. Since the sub-soil is rooted in the same manner as overburden, the result is distribution of lime to a good depth. Large stones which appear after sub-soil rooting are removed. Top soil is spread in the same manner as sub-soil.

The timing of soil spreading is important; if it is carried out under wet conditions, rutting will occur and the spread will be uneven. It is preferable to have top soil graded sufficiently early in the year for grass seed to be sown and some growth established to control soil erosion by water and wind. Frequently sub-soil is spread in autumn and the areas left to weather for the winter. Limestone is added the following spring, and the subsequent rooting takes out surface irregularities which have been created during the winter.

On moorland or peaty areas, the surface layer of fibrous peat and sandy materials will be spread. As far as possible the proportion of peat and clay in the surface layer should be low in relation to sandy matter, or there will be a tendency for soft wet patches to occur, promoting the growth of moisture-loving plants. Supervision of the materials being taken from dumps can help to improve the surface mix.

Agricultural treatment
Soil which has been stored in dumps for several months may appear normal when lifted and re-spread, but in fact it will have changed in nature very considerably. The soil will be acid and short of nitrogen and phosphates, but additionally it will be lifeless and without structure. Compaction in mound excludes air from the soil, with the resultant loss of aerobic bacteria which promote the breakdown of vegetable matter into humus and assist in fixing nitrogen. The structurally changed soil when

re-spread is restrictive to water movement, further inhibiting air movement and bacterial growth. Without proper treatment the surface soil would become a hard crust in summer and waterlogged in winter, during which period the soil temperature would be lowered, resulting in a late growth the following spring. The answer is to stimulate growth, in spring and summer, of both root and top. The penetration of living roots breaks the soil and aids air movement, which in turn starts the action of micro-organisms on the dead roots. Over a period this leads to the formation of humus, return of an earthworm population, and restoration of fertility. Treatment and management of restored agricultural land therefore requires specialized knowledge, enthusiastic interest and patience. Top-soil will usually receive 3 to 4 tons of ground limestone per acre in the first spring or sowing period. Cultivation by ploughing and harrowing will follow to produce a seed bed into which a compound fertilizer is worked at a rate of 4 cwt per acre (500 kg/ha). This may be followed with a top dressing of basic slag at a rate of 1 ton per acre ($2\frac{1}{2}$ tonnes per hectare). The surface is then re-harrowed, rolled and is ready for seeding to grass.

The seed mix and quantity per acre have been varied experimentally according to soil and site location. Between 22 and 48 lb per acre* have been used, the average quantity per acre being higher in Scotland where the growing season is shorter. The object is to have seed with both early and late growth, in sufficient quantity to establish a good sole with close rooting. White clover is usually introduced because this plant has nitrogen-fixing properties useful in restoring soil fertility. On heavier soils a good pasture has been obtained from a mixture of cocksfoot, fescues, timothy and clover, the mixed strains of grass giving herbage growth through the season. A general mix used in some cases is:*

Perennial ryeglass (early)	8 lb per acre
Perennial ryegrass (leafy)	8 „ „ „
Italian ryegrass	4 „ „ „
Timothy	4 „ „ „
Cocksfoot (early)	4 „ „ „
Cocksfoot (late)	4 „ „ „
Rough-stalked meadow grass	1 „ „ „
Red clover (late)	3 „ „ „
Wild white clover N.Z.	$1\frac{1}{2}$ „ „ „
Wild white clover Kent	$\frac{1}{2}$ „ „ „
	38 lb per acre

Recently an exposed wet site on a north-facing slope and with medium

* 20 cwt = 1 ton = 2240 lb   2·47 acres = 1 hectare
  1 short ton = 2000 lb
  1 metric ton = 1 tonne = 1000 kg = 2204 lb
  1 lb/acre = 1·12 kg/ha

soil was treated with $1\frac{1}{2}$ tons per acre ground lime, 5 cwt per acre ground mineral phosphate, and 4 cwt per acre compound fertilizers (23N/11P/11K). The land was then seeded at 32 lb per acre with the following mix: Perennial ryegrass (early) 6 lb per acre, Midsummer ryegrass 8 lb, Late ryegrass 5 lb, Italian ryegrass 4 lb, Timothy 6 lb, Wild white clover 2 lb, Smooth-stalked meadow grass 1 lb. The result was a good growth.

In 1974 the southern slope of a bank of sandy sub-soil was seeded to improve its appearance. An application was made of compound fertilizers ($12/12\frac{1}{2}/18$) at $4\frac{1}{2}$ cwt per acre, followed by grass seeding (per acre) of a mixture: Perennial ryegrass (Danish early) 20 lb, Creeping red fescue (Canadian) 14 lb, Wild white clover Kent 0·5 lb.

When a reasonable growth has been established, controlled grazing by sheep and cattle is allowed under supervision of the agricultural field officers, who restrict the number of beasts to suit ground and grass conditions. To do this, the land may be parcelled by erection of permanent fencing or stone walling, or movable electric fencing may be used. Ideally, main ditches are dug before final soil cultivation—but if there is no drainage problem, and the restored area is small, ditching and fencing may be carried out after grass has been established. Over a period of up to 5 years, compound fertilizer, basic slag or nitro chalk, will be used as necessary to restore the soil fertility. By that time the land will have settled and, if desirable, under-drainage will be laid. The restored drainage runs will be cultivated and re-seeded; in many instances the entire area is ploughed and re-seeded to permanent pasture. Design of the under-drainage scheme is carried out by the Ministry (or Department) of Agriculture and the work completed by a specialist contractor. The spacing between lateral runs depends on ground conditions, but 10 metres is normal. The pipes may be clay or plastic. When there will be a tendency to scour, as where leader drains enter an open ditch, proper head walls and stone pitching are constructed.

Restoration to forestry or woodland
As an ancillary to agricultural restoration, it is frequently desirable to plant small woods or shelter belts. It may be possible to do such planting at an early stage of opencast working on parts of the site not required for excavation or dump room. In that case the trees will be well established by the time normal restoration is finalized. Otherwise, shelter-belt planting will be on land restored to agricultural standards and seeded with grass. The area is ploughed and fenced to be rabbit-proof, and (depending on soil condition) may be sub-soiled to assist drainage. As we might expect, birch and alder grow fairly quickly, whilst sycamore, red oak, larch and Corsican pine can be considered to be reasonably successful. Sitka spruce

transplants (12″–18″) have been planted in Ayrshire and will be used largely for an area in Lanarkshire where the atmosphere is clean, summer tends to be wet, and the restored surface mixture of sand, peat and light clay will be a metre in depth, giving good rooting potential.

Most of the land restored for tree planting is owned by the Forestry Commission who, as agents to the Board, plant and maintain the forests at the Board's expense for up to 5 years, after which the land and plantation is handed back to the Commission. Where the land is owned by the Board it is usually sold to the Commission after physical restoration, then leased back for the 5-year period to allow plantations to be established, with the Board bearing the cost. On expiry of the lease, the Forestry Commission has an afforested parcel of land.

Taking a bonus from opencast mining

Opencast mining for coal takes place where the seams are shallow. If mining has been carried out in the past, the scars of that industry may still exist in the shape of waste tips, shafts, mineral railway formations, slurry lagoons and subsided land. So far restoration to agriculture or forestry has been described, because the fear of the environmentalist is that land will be laid waste by opencasting; that fear is unfounded. A large earth-moving operation such as opencast mining, carried out in an old industrial district, could also take waste land and make it attractive and usable, and that is exactly what is done wherever the right circumstances exist. If such dereliction occurs within a site boundary, it is cleared away, and in many instances the boundary is extended to include nearby disused tips. Old buildings are demolished, foundations lifted and railway forma-tions removed, or filled, depending on whether they are on bank or in cutting.

It is an expensive business entirely to remove a colliery waste tip. The normal practice is to reduce it in height to an acceptable level, and then re-shape it to merge into the surrounding landscape. There is seldom sufficient top soil available to permit even a thin spread over the reclaimed land. In most cases it has to be covered with a layer of soil-making material conserved from the opencast excavation. Waste material from the cleared area is well buried in the backfill, as a useful "imported" addition which will permit final levels to be raised.

Tips which are liable to spontaneous combustion are a special problem. The material within the tip is very hot and bursts into flame when exposed, sending a fine hot dust into the air. The task has to be tackled with as many motor scrapers as practical. The drivers require face masks and are given frequent rest intervals. Tyres may catch fire, therefore under very hot conditions tracked vehicles drawing scraper boxes have to be used. Dozers must be in attendance to train-off burning material or to push scrapers out of areas where they are tending to sink.

Sub-soil used as a carpet material can be sown with grass seed, but it is essential to have an analysis taken of the top section of spread waste and of the sub-soil. Very low pH-values are normal in such waste tips, and the acid level cannot always be corrected by heavy liming. Other minerals such as manganese, copper and zinc are also likely to be present. A layer of soil, however thin, is a distinct advantage in all cases, and is essential in many. Peat which is itself acidic may well be found on poorly drained land around old tips, but is not a suitable material to use on the reshaped mound surface, particularly if the latter is composed of unburnt shaley coal. The resultant mix will defy a heavy programme of liming. On an East of Scotland waste tip with a pH of 2·8, about 4 inches of top soil, recovered from building development a few miles away, was sufficient to encourage a good take from a grass seed mix, with fertilizer (applied at the time of sowing) at a rate supplying 60 units of N, P, and K per acre. The seed mixture, used at 47 lb per acre, was:

25 lb	S.23 Ryegrass
10 lb	Creeping red fescue
5 lb	Smooth-stalked meadow grass
2 lb	Crested dogtail
2 lb	Rough-stalked meadow grass
2 lb	White clover (New Zealand)
1 lb	Wild white clover (Kent)

A site now being worked at Cowdenbeath, Fife, will produce 2 million tons of coal, followed by agricultural restoration of 337 acres, reclaiming 220 acres of derelict land, removing 4 disused pit heaps and reshaping another which stood 50 metres high, removing 7 coal slurry ponds, making safe 38 old shafts and constructing a consolidated strip 1500 metres in length on which the highway authority plans to build a trunk road or motorway. The road would otherwise have to pass over unstable marshy areas and sections where underground voids from old coal mining exist. The cost of these extra restoration works is to be borne by the opencast mining operation which will still represent a profitable venture for the National Coal Board. Restoration will be enhanced by tree planting, the scale of which will be agreed with the local authority.

The project demonstrates that a large-scale operation provides scope for generous landscaping, giving long-term benefits to the district. The coaling period will be five years, during which all major earthworks will be completed, leaving a further five years for land rehabilitation, forestry, construction of public walks, and perhaps of a recreation area.

Planning for changed use of land depends upon the ownership of land and chattels. Should the owner of an area in the middle of other land want his portion restored and fenced as it had been, the Board must abide by his wishes and has no powers compulsorily to acquire his interest. If the local authority, in the interest of the people it serves, wishes the Board to alter the use of land it does not own, that authority will probably first have to buy the surface under a compulsory purchase order.

There are unique opportunities in opencast mining to provide a changed landscape for new uses. Where shallow coal reserves lie near an inhabited area, there is often particular need for recreational areas. Golf courses can be, and have been, made on restored land, working to the design and specification of experts. Football pitches have been made in districts where there is an increasing need to provide youths with sports facilities. Pleasant walks through woodland can be made; by recontouring flat land, a more pleasing visual amenity can be produced. Public highways which are removed during opencast working can be reinstated on a different route, giving greater safety for modern traffic.

In some areas washland has been eliminated by revising levels or building flood banks. Where such action would cause additional flooding downstream, the washland has been reduced in size by providing an equivalent water tankage in a channel forming a backwater to the main stream. The sides of the channel can be stone-pitched where necessary, to prevent damage to the banks which are constructed at a safe angle. Trees can be planted along the tops of banks; footpaths and seats can be installed.

Farming

To amalgamate two or more farms in order to make one viable unit is not uncommon, but it is seldom possible to combine farms and re-plan completely the internal layout to suit a fresh appraisal of agricultural economy. Such opportunities have been presented by two opencast sites in Scotland, and the Department of Agriculture and Fisheries for Scotland are advising on all aspects of the projects.

In one instance, two neighbouring Ayrshire farms were purchased by the Board in order to mine a good-quality bituminous coal. Farm No. 1, with approximately 400 acres of rough grazing and 40 acres of normal grazing, carried around 380 upland sheep. Farm No. 2 had 40 acres of mowing grass and 140 acres of grazing, stocked with 38 dairy cattle, 60 other cattle and 90 lowland sheep. When restored, the single unit will have a new farmhouse and steading sited in a position suitable for control of the 620 acres. An agricultural worker's cottage will be built, and the internal farm roads will be improved and extended. A water supply will be laid on, and drainage will be considerably improved. An easily managed mixed-stock farm, probably with a dairy herd, will result from adjusting internal field boundaries in relation to the roads and buildings.

In the second case, three small West Lothian farms with dilapidated and unsuitable buildings formed the site of an opencast mine, now under agricultural rehabilitation. These farms, with areas of 98, 130 and 150 acres, were not viable units. They are now to be amalgamated and re-equipped with modern buildings and piped water. The agricultural use will not alter, but farming will be more efficient, and the living conditions more attractive, to those employed on the land.

These schemes are being financed by the opencast profits, assisted where appropriate by grants, approved in principle, under the Farm Amalgamation and Boundaries Scheme 1970. Mineral extraction and agriculture may appear to be totally opposed interests but, by planned consultation, the farmer can provide improvements to the land not otherwise likely to be achieved.

Open-pit uses

The first consideration is that the pit walls should be safe. Where the excavation is in rock, it may be necessary to use pre-splitting techniques when blasting, in order to obtain a clean break along the desired line.

Old quarries, worked into a hillside, frequently occur in areas of natural beauty. Perhaps they could be utilized for car parks, overnight stopping points for caravans, or picnic areas with car access. Where public access can be useful, as in any of those suggestions, the stability of the rock face is an important safety aspect. A face liable to break should have fencing to keep persons away from the base of the wall; it should be provided with safety benches, or be netted. Use of a minimum amount of soil, grass seed and shrubs can, with imagination, transform a derelict quarry into an attractive useful area, especially if it can be equipped with toilet facilities, a piped water supply—and the ever-necessary waste bins.

Wet gravel pits can often be landscaped into leisure centres for water sports, or nature reserves for wild fowl. Once again, if the public are to have access, their safety must be considered, and shore lines made so that a person does not step from the bank into deep water, but has to wade on a gradual decline until out of depth.

Disposal of waste by local authorities and industry is an increasing problem. An open pit, kept dry by pumping, can be of great value as a reception area for non-toxic material and processed waste. If this is to be the after-use, it is worth conserving overburden and sub-soil around the pit edge, so that there can be a final covering which will support plant growth.

Licensed opencast sites

There are instances where coal is extracted by private persons operating with a licence granted by the National Coal Board under Section 36 of the Coal Industry Nationalisation Act 1946, as amended by Section 46 of the Opencast Coal Act 1958. The Board is empowered to permit the digging and carrying away of coal disturbed as part of another operation, such as excavation for foundation to a building or road. Under Sub-Section 36(2)(b) of the 1946 Act, the Board can licence "the working of coal present among other minerals that appears to the Board to be of such small value that the working thereof is unlikely to be undertaken otherwise than as ancillary to the workings of those minerals", and by Sub-Section 36(2)(c) it can "permit the licensing of coal won by opencast methods where the amount to be won is, in the Board's opinion not likely greatly to exceed 25,000 tons". The Opencast Executive deal with grant of licence under these two Sub-Sections, but permission to work the site has to be obtained (usually by the operator) from the local planning authority, who make conditions of working and restoration. When licensing the extraction of coal, the Executive insert clauses which make compliance with planning conditions a licence obligation. In addition, the licensee is required to provide a guarantee bond to ensure there will be money available for completion of those requirements. The amount of bond is calculated by the Executive, and normally covers the anticipated cost of full restoration of land. If a man builds a house without planning permission, the planning authority can demolish it; but if that man digs a hole and extracts a mineral, the planning position is not so easy. Should the man become bankrupt, does the authority fill the hole for him? The Board's approach, where disturbance of coal is part of a private project for mineral extraction, gives protection to the local amenities, and the Town and Country Planning Acts are strengthened in a practical way.

The present and the future of opencast coal in the United Kingdom

How much does this method of producing coal utilize land, and for what tonnage? The current contribution of opencast is around 10 million tons per annum and, to achieve this, approximately 38,000 acres of good, bad and indifferent land are occupied. Since restoration is progressive, some land is being released whilst other areas are being taken over. Between the years 1970 and 1974 over 1400 acres of derelict land have been reclaimed in association with opencast mining. Surely this is optimum use of land resources. It is now considered essential that opencast produces 15 million tons a year for a period of several years, but this does not mean a 50% increase in land occupation. The value of coal is now sufficient to allow it to be won at a higher ratio and at greater depth from a slightly increased surface area.

Complexities arise from choice of excavation method, selection of mechanical plant to suit the task, preparation of coal for the market, and road or rail dispatch. However, we are here concerned mainly with environmental effect, reclamation and restoration, not with the technicalities of mining and marketing opencast coal.

Inevitably one wonders about cost, but in the present inflationary situation where costs escalate erratically, there is little point in quoting a sum of money for any particular aspect of work. It may be more useful if costs are given as an approximate percentage of the average saleable value of industrial bituminous coal. The physical task of filling the void in a normal opencast mine will, of course, depend on the volume of material to be brought from mounds, and the distance involved. The cost therefore can vary from 1–10% of the bituminous coal value, replacement of sub-soil and top soil can represent another 8–10%. These are included in the contractor's rate for producing coal and not usually paid for as separate items. Agricultural rehabilitation, i.e. cultivation, fencing, drainage by ditch and pipe, water supply to fields, and miscellaneous items, account for 3–6% of the coal proceeds. Providing the operation is planned in advance, with physical reclamation and restoration in mind, so that the necessary cost of that part of the task is kept to a minimum, agricultural land can be returned to full or improved use for a relatively small sum. It must be remembered, however, that climate, location and availability of suitable surface materials as growing media play a major role in deciding how successful a land restoration will be.

Opinions expressed in this chapter are the author's and are not necessarily those of the National Coal Board.

FURTHER READING

R. T. Arguile (1974), *Clearance of Dereliction in Industrial Areas*, The Institution of Municipal Engineers.

H. L. Nichols Jnr. (1969), *Moving the Earth*, North Castle. Covers all aspects of excavation and machinery used.

Land Utilization and Reclamation in the Mining Industry 1930–71. United States Department of the Interior. (Bureau of Mines Information Circular/1974.)

CHAPTER THREE

PIT HEAP INTO PASTURE

NATURAL AND ARTIFICIAL REVEGETATION OF COAL MINE WASTE

J. A. RICHARDSON

Introduction

In the course of the eighteenth century, the population in Britain doubled from around 6 million in 1702 to 11 million in 1801; in the following 50 years, the population doubled again. Towards the end of the nineteenth century, the excess of births over deaths in England was 14 per thousand of the population and in Germany it was 11. In Europe, the survival of more infants and the prolongation of the average life, which marked off modern times from the past, were largely due to the developing science of preventive medicine, in which inoculation, vaccination, hygiene, sanitation, midwifery and the founding of the voluntary hospitals and dispensaries played a part. The possibility of the overpopulation of Europe, which terrified the contemporaries of Malthus, was diminished by the emigration of millions of Europeans to the relatively empty lands overseas.

Inevitably, the population explosion which started in Europe in the middle of the eighteenth century, spread in the twentieth century to Asia and Africa, where the dramatic elimination of diseases such as malaria produced a steep rise in the world's population. From around the 1000 million mark in 1850, the rise had been rapid to 2500 million in 1950, with a forecast, based on present trends, of 6500 million in 2000 (25 years from now). By 2050 there could be 12000 million people on earth. Until now, man by his discoveries and inventiveness has been able partly to conceal the truth that the supply of natural resources, especially of open land, may soon run out. However, the evidence of numbers and available space shows that man cannot survive on earth if he continues to multiply as he is doing at present, without a lowering of his living standards.

Diminution of the quality of life is the exact opposite of traditional hopes for the future. Man's aim must now be to close the gaps in living standards by raising the quality of life in the underdeveloped countries. The nations of the world must control their populations in order to achieve this goal. If population control is accepted, there will be an opportunity to improve the environment; but this will require careful planning and managing of resources.

The problems on a world scale are enormous, and so far there has been little real attempt at population and resource planning. However, the incentive to find solutions is man's own survival. He must find ways to control his numbers, and he must devise methods of enhancing the environment and not debasing it. Some countries are overpopulated in respect of their resources; some places in the world are over-congested; and in all countries many localities are being destroyed by pressure of numbers. Man must arrange to husband all his resources and, according to reports from the United Nations and its major agencies, he must act speedily to reduce the frightening pace of world-wide pollution. It is heartening to know that leaders of society, governments and ordinary citizens, have heard and responded to the danger signals, and that at least some parts of the great problem are being actively investigated. Any local scheme to make more land available for agriculture, amenity or recreation, or to remove unsightly features in the landscape, must be seen as a gain in the fight to produce and maintain a high-quality environment. In many countries there has been a marked change in attitude towards preserving landscape from industrial spoilation; and both planning regulations and public opinion impose such restraints on pollution that industry is being forced to take remedial action.

A splendid example of this welcome change of heart is afforded by two separate mining activities in the Cleveland area of north-east England. Ironstone mining began there on a large scale in 1845, and it flourished for about a hundred years, during which time some 600 million tons of ore were produced. Teesside became one of Europe's leading iron and steel-producing regions, and Middlesbrough, its chief town, grew from 100 inhabitants in 1830 to 150,000 in 1930. When the mines finally closed down, huge heaps of dark brown waste stretched eastwards across the country in a broad band 12 miles long, from Ayton (7 miles south of Middlesbrough) to the North Sea just beyond the town of Loftus. Many of these spoil heaps still remain in the derelict mining villages—grim relics of single-minded industrialism which have long offended the eye and polluted the air with grit.

In the 1960s plans were made by Imperial Chemical Industries and other international companies to sink deep mines in Cleveland, for the purpose of extracting deposits rich in potassium salts. Government backing was given to the Boulby Potash Mine, situated 3 miles south of Loftus and one mile north of Staithes in the North York Moors National Park. Strong arguments in support of Government approval for the scheme were Britain's world trade and the promise of over 600 jobs in Cleveland, where the unemployment was about 10%. Clearly this mine, which had a planned yearly output of over 2 million tons of mined material, possessed the same potential for debasing the environment as the large ironstone workings that lay a few miles away to the north. However, in this case there were modern planning laws, backed by public opinion and an enlightened management, to ensure that there was better control of pollution risks than had existed in the days of ironstone mining.

The final plan of the whole site, embracing the shafts, ore-storage, waste disposal, processing and other buildings, which were prepared by landscape architects and approved by all concerned, went much further than providing mere cosmetic treatment. To begin with, the visual nuisance caused by large pithead installations, was relieved by siting the mine in a bowl-shaped tract of ground at the foot of Boulby Hill (680 feet, 207 m) on the south-west side and near to Easington Beck. The buildings were concealed as far as possible behind a bank of earth, for which about 400,000 tons of material were moved. At suitable points in and around the site over 20,000 deciduous and evergreen trees were planted to blend with the surrounding countryside. The line of the roofs was successfully made unobtrusive, and the pair of tall chimneys (built to nearly 300 feet (90 m) in order to disperse the smoke) was so elegant that, if they did not actually elicit praise, they turned away any criticism.

The mine waste, estimated at about 1 million tons per year, was removed from the site as slurry and taken in a long underground pipe to be discharged in the sea about a mile off-shore. As a further safeguard, planning consent was only given on the strict condition that discharge of effluent into the sea would be stopped if there was reason to suspect damage to marine life and the local crab and lobster fisheries. Furthermore, the company agreed that no compensation would be payable to them if the Secretary of State for the Environment made such an order.

Thus, the Boulby Potash Mine amply demonstrates that in Britain there has now been achieved a situation where industry has to think seriously about the pollution it causes and its obligation to clean up its own mess, even at great cost. While this is not satisfactory as a long-term ecological answer, and there is still the legacy of past industrial dereliction to be eliminated, it must be regarded as an important step towards cleaner land.

The Boulby Potash Mine is an excellent example of the need for economic growth not being allowed to overrule completely all effects on the environment. Only time will tell, but 2 years after production started, it seemed that the company and its advisers on one hand, and the Government and the local planning officers on the other hand, had co-operated so successfully that over 2 million tons of rock could be mined annually without debasing the countryside.

It is doubtful if the early miners anywhere who dug for iron, gold, silver, copper, lead, aluminium, coal, china clay, sulphur, and so on ever gave thought for posterity. They left waste material scattered at random around the workings and about the sites they abandoned when the task of winning the minerals became too difficult or uneconomic. The world's population was small, land was plentiful, and man could afford to be profligate with the earth's resources. The dereliction caused in the coal-mining areas in England, Scotland and Wales was very similar to that in the eastern United States, in Germany, Czechoslovakia and elsewhere.

In Britain, as in other countries, the earliest coal mines were usually driven into the sides of hills and valleys at points where the seams out-cropped at the surface. Later, shallow pits (20 feet deep) were dug down to the coal; and then, to reach the lower seams of coal, vertical shafts were sunk to about 80 feet below the surface. In both cases, the coal was taken from around the base of the shaft to an extent that was limited by the distances that air could circulate freely. In the early days there was a lack of suitable illuminants, and it was necessary to tolerate the increased foulness of the atmosphere caused by the primitive lamps— or to work, as some did, by the feeble phosphorescent glow of putrefying fish. When the workings at one place were stopped because of bad ventilation, new ones were started up again at the nearest convenient site nearby. The waste material from the collieries was usually dumped around the pithead, but the amount was so small by modern quantities that it had little effect on the countryside. To-day most of these small pit heaps have been dispersed and incorporated in adjoining farmland, and those that remain support tiny woodlands consisting chiefly of *Acer pseudoplatanus* (sycamore), *Crataegus monogyna* (hawthorn), *Sambucus nigra* (elder), *Rosa* spp. (rose) and *Rubus* spp. (bramble) (see p. 85).

In England after the year 1600 there was a slow but steady increase in the demand for coal for use in factories and smelters and for export, as well as for an increasing household market; this rate of growth of coalmining continued until just before the Industrial Revolution. The outstanding industrial innovation of the time was the substitution of coke for charcoal in the production of pig iron and castings. However, Abraham Darby's discovery at Coalbrookdale, Shropshire in 1709 was slow to catch on, and the increase in coal production was not greatly affected for some time. Moreover, charcoal had still to be used to convert the coke-smelted pig into bar iron that was used for making tools and machinery. It was nearly 80 years later that Henry Cort's method provided the solution which freed the forge masters of their dependence on the woodlands, just as Darby's had the furnace owners.

Coal was now in colossal demand as the chief industrial fuel for the production of iron and steel, for firing the boilers of steam engines in factories, workshops and mills, and on the railways. The ingenious devices that flowed from the technical revolution were used to bring about improvements in mine lighting, ventilation, deep-shaft construction, underground drainage and other aspects of mining, and the result was a further boost to coal production. There was a correspondingly huge increase in the amount of mine waste, and this was heaped on to the land in mounds, ridges and cones—usually near to the colliery and to the houses of the miners. In north-east England, the Durham and Northumberland coalfield has been worked on a larger scale and for a longer time than any other in Britain.

Because of access by sea to the London market, the Durham and Northumberland coalfield quickly became the largest and best-developed area of production, and in 1700 the annual output was just under half of the British total; only in 1900 did the proportion drop to one fifth. In the last 200 years it has produced about 6000 million tons of saleable coal. During the same time over 28,000 million tons of dirty water have been poured into the rivers and over 1000 million tons of mine waste have been piled up on the land. On the coast of east Durham, beautiful Magnesian Limestone denes have been used as waste tips and, when these were filled in, the dirt was dropped into the sea and on to the beaches. In large areas of Durham and Northumberland, the landscape had been badly marked by the waste heaps and other paraphernalia of mining; as the old mines became worked out they lay neglected and choked by their own rubbish. Surprisingly, up to about 1955, there seem to have been very few attempts to control the disposal of waste with a view to ameliorating the general ugliness that spread across the landscape; consequently Gibraltars made of coal waste and slag towered over the houses in mining towns. Because of their heights, the heaps are visible for many miles and, in spite of the relatively small areas they occupy, they loom up as depressing eyesores over large areas of the countryside. To make conditions even worse, many of the heaps began spontaneously to burn, and then the air around was polluted with sulphurous fumes. These conditions, which were a feature of north-east England, are found in other deep-mine coalfields elsewhere in Britain, in Europe and in the

United States.

To many people it would seem that an obvious method of preventing new pollution of the environment by colliery spoil would be to return the waste material back undergound and stow it in worked-out parts of the mine. The advantages of this procedure are not in dispute and if, as a guide, we allow 1 ton of waste for 5 tons of saleable coal, there would certainly be no lack of space. When entire coal seams are removed, there is a grave risk of land subsidence, with untold damage to roads, bridges, railways, houses, factories, sewers, water pipes, etc., as well as to arable and park land; and the coal industry is well aware of the financial implications of such occurrences. In order to support the surface and avoid subsidence, large pillars of coal are left in the workings. It has been argued that many millions of tons of this sterilized coal could be won, provided another method of support could be found, and the case for using the waste material as stowage has been strongly urged. Nevertheless, in Britain there has never been any legislation to provide for the back-filling of waste into worked-out parts of mines, and consequently the waste has been raised to the surface for disposal. There is no complete stowage in use in Britain at the present time. The management argue that old mines were not laid out to take waste back underground, and state that in any case the cost in new mines would be greater than the industry could reasonably be expected to bear. In spite of these difficulties, the technique of stowage has been developed and extensively used in the Ruhr coalfield in Germany.

A further seemingly obvious means of waste disposal is to fill in the huge excavations left by the surface extraction of sand, gravel, limestone, sandstone, clay, etc., said to amount to something of the order of 200 million tons yearly in Britain. Since the output of colliery waste currently amounts only to about 25 million tons, there ought to be space to accommodate the newly produced spoil and so prevent any accumulation of shale in heaps on the surface. Furthermore, it would seem that substantial inroads could be made to old spoil heaps. However, it seems that transport costs and certain technical difficulties associated with surface extraction are such that, at the present time, only a few million tons a year are removed to holes in the ground.

There is no accumulation of colliery waste from certain large coastal mines in Durham and Northumberland, because the whole of the output is taken out to sea in special ships and dumped on to the sea bed. Domestic refuse from seaside towns has long been disposed of in this way, and the waste is tipped overboard far enough out to sea to avoid polluting the beaches. There could be over 1 million tons of shale per year tipped at sea in this fashion.

A more valuable method for getting rid of colliery waste is to use it in major roadworks and other civil-engineering activities. Whereas the red shale from burnt-out heaps has long been used for this purpose, it has recently been accepted that unburnt black shale may also be a valuable bulk filling material in highway construction, provided it is well compacted and sealed. For example, there are several places in Northumberland, Durham, Yorkshire, Lancashire and Nottinghamshire where new motorways run through the coalfields, and pit heap spoil is readily available; and, of course, there is the added bonus for the community of improvement to the environment by removing the heaps. Although in Britain only about 10 million tons of shale have so far been used for road foundations, it is possible that in future greater quantities can be hidden from sight in this way.

When due allowance has been made for shale disposed of in these various ways, the position seems to be that there is still at least 2000 million tons of shale lying in pit heaps in the coalfields of Britain and, at the present production level of deep-mined coal, another 12 million tons of spoil is added each year.

Large pit heaps, whether they are in ridges or are cone-shaped, make an ugly intrusion into the landscape and, of course, this is exaggerated in flat country such as parts of the British coalfields in Midlothian, Northumberland, Yorkshire and Nottinghamshire. Most observers agree that it is the black and grey colour, rather than the shape, that makes the greater contribution to the general ugliness of heaps, and the practice of detopping tall conical pit heaps makes only a slight improvement to the environment. However, for people who live in mining areas, as distinct from those who pass through by motor-car or in the train, it is not the visual pollution that makes life intolerable but the air pollution.

A 2-million-ton shale heap on the doorstep means that clean air is unknown, except in winter during a snowfall; for most of the time in dry weather the air is filled with dust that blinds the eyes, stings the face and pollutes the respiratory passages. It is a surprising fact that pneumoconiosis, a serious disease of the lungs which affects face workers in deep coal mines, has never been found in other underground mine workers or in surfacemen concerned with loading and transporting the coal and shales. Nor have there been any cases of the illness amongst the ordinary inhabitants of mining towns who live in the shadows of waste heaps and coal storage yards. Nevertheless, bare pitheaps add a great amount of material to the polluted air of industrial areas, and shale dust must be reckoned as part of industrial pollution.

What is not in doubt is the much higher incidence of chronic bronchitis (the English disease) and bronchogenic carcinoma in mining areas than in rural areas. Taking those in England and Wales suffering from these diseases, the difference in numbers between industrial and rural patients is much greater than the difference between smoking and non-smoking patients. Notwithstanding the fact that these diseases kill five times as many people as the motor-car, and deaths from them are six times greater in mining areas than in seaside resorts, there has been virtually no consistent lobby against pit heaps on the grounds of a health hazard.

When the heaps are clothed with vegetation, the dust problem disappears immediately and, at the same time, the appearance is greatly improved when green and fawn replace black and grey.

Natural colonization

By examining the events and processes that occur during the natural spread of plants on to spoil heaps, information useful as a guide for planting in full reclamation schemes has been obtained. In temperate lands, most waste ground which has not some serious physical or chemical defect, is successfully invaded by plants from the surrounding countryside. Under very favourable conditions, on many colliery spoil heaps a tree and grass cover can become established in about 40 years, and then gradually the heaps become assimilated into the landscape. It seems that normally most non-toxic spoil heaps, e.g. those in County Durham, achieve some sort of vegetative cover after sixty years, but clearly the nature of the plant community and the speed with which it develops depend on a number of inter-related factors. Prominent influences will be the composition of the spoil heap, its shape, slope and aspect, and the rate of weathering of the various components. Then the air and water content, the temperature of the surface layers, and the presence or absence of organic matter, nutrients and toxic substances will play some part in determining the extent of the colonization of the heap by pioneer species. Finally, the nature of the plant population in the adjacent countryside is important, particularly the habitat requirements and the means of seed dispersal of the plants concerned.

The shape of pit heaps

In the early days of mining, when land values were low and mechanization was less highly developed, the heaps were usually between 15 and 20 feet high and in the form of mounds or ridges. Both the mounds and the ridges were flat-topped. Only occasionally were several mounds found together, but very often multiple ridges occurred. When it became common practice to deposit waste material from aerial conveyors, razor-backed spoil heaps were formed, and later, when it was important to be more economical as regards the amount of land covered, the method of making large conical heaps was adopted. These were asymmetrical, with a more gentle slope up which the hopper travelled on rails, and a steeper side down which the spoil was tipped; they were commonly up to 200 feet in height and might contain several millions of tons of material.

The height and form of spoil heaps affects their ability to support plants in at least five important ways:

(1) It could be argued that the conical heaps which commonly exceed 100 feet in height will *intercept greater numbers of wind-blown seeds* than the low mounds of 20 feet. If this were the case, then under favourable soil conditions, we might expect a fairly rapid appearance on the heaps of representative species from the surrounding countryside.

(2) *The slope affects the evaporation rate* from the surface layers of the heap in so far as, on the south-facing slopes of a conical heap, the surface is for long periods at right angles to the direction of the sun's radiation. This fact, coupled with the high absorption coefficient of the black shales, results in much higher temperatures than would exist on horizontal and lighter-coloured surfaces. Surface temperature differences of 10 °C are not uncommon between the north and the south-facing slopes, and when these temperature differences are maintained for five hours appreciable differences occur in moisture content of the surface layers.

(3) *The stability of the surface* of the heaps is bound up with the process of weathering, and also with the slope of the surface. In the case of heaps composed largely of fine debris, shallow mounds with a small slope, e.g. 30°, become stable much sooner than tall conical heaps with a slope of more than 40°. When a heap contains a large amount of coarse shales, slopes up to 43° become stable within a few months of final tipping. It is surprising to find that in heaps of this sort, especially when the shales are quickly weathered, their height has little effect on either the time required for stability or the final angle of rest that is achieved. Clearly, until stability does occur, the casualties resulting from snapped roots and buried seedlings caused by a shifting surface layer will retard the rate of colonization.

(4) *The rate of run-off of water* from the surface will control the quantity of the small-sized soil-forming particles that are lost during heavy rainfall. Run-off is governed by the texture of the surface layers and the slope of the surface. With flat-topped ridges and mounds in the course of weathering, the permeability of the surface layers to water may become reduced to such an extent that, during rainfall, water first collects in pools and later runs off down the slopes in minor torrents. It has been demonstrated that, although the amount of erosion on bare slopes is largely determined by the degree of slope, the length of the slope

may be important under certain circumstances; and it seems the length of slope is more important in heavy rainfall than in light.

The removal by water of the fine newly-dispersed particles takes place (a) to the bottom of the slope in heavy rain or (b) to some distance beneath the surface level in light rain. The result, so far as the surface is concerned, is in many cases to leave behind a loose layer of thin plates of shale, which makes a poor seed-bed. Not only does this material provide little or no anchorage for the roots, but its water-retaining capacity is extremely small.

(5) On high exposed spoil heaps, a considerable amount of *fine material is removed by high winds* and this increases the total losses of soil-forming matter. Of course, the loss of soil-forming particles from spoil heaps is influenced by factors other than their size and shape. For example, the rainfall intensity and distribution in any district is important, and so is the infiltration capacity of the soil. When a cover of vegetation has formed over the surface, the erosion is reduced to a very low amount. This may be due, in the first place, to the protection the leafy shoots give against the beating action of the rain. In a heavy downpour, the pores of a bare permeable soil may be reduced so much under the impact of the raindrops that the infiltration capacity is impaired and run-off occurs; the denser the plant cover becomes, the less likely are changes in porosity.

Secondly, the effect of plant roots in the soil is to promote an open but well-held structure by the formation of granules and old root channels. As the amount of organic matter in the surface layers of a clayey shale heap increases, the texture will become more open, and the infiltration capacity will increase. For a soil composed largely of hard platy shales, the presence of organic matter in the form of living and dead roots increases granulation and surface stability. At the same time, the infiltration rate is reduced to a level which both allows heavy rains to penetrate without run-off and also allows sufficient water to be retained for plant growth. Finally, even when the rainfall exceeds the infiltration capacity of a soil, the presence of a network of roots and shoots checks erosion by slowing up the rate at which water travels down the sides of the spoil heap. When the rate of run-off is decreased, there is more time for infiltration, and hence the total run-off is decreased.

Weathering of pit-heap material

(1) *The rate of disintegration.* Observations made on a large number of spoil heaps suggest that the progress of the breakdown of the large shales, rejected coal, clay and sandstone which lie at the surface of many of them

roughly follows a sigmoid curve. During the first nine months after tipping, the rate of weathering is slow and involves the scouring of the softer laminations in the shales by rain and wind and ice action, so that eventually the intact boulders begin to shatter along the bedding planes. Once this process has commenced, the rate of disintegration accelerates, and in the following 3–4 months there is an increase in the amount of smaller particles ($<$ 2 mm) present. The final breakdown into the smallest-sized material ($<$ 0·02 mm) proceeds at a slower rate.

In addition to the physical agents of weathering, chemical processes also play a part in the breakdown of the solid rock into soil-forming particles. For example, the oxidation of iron sulphide to form iron sulphate and sulphuric acid tends to break up the shales containing such deposits. The acid so formed further accelerates disintegration by acting on the binding substances present in the laminations.

It has been found that, when disintegration has proceeded to a point where about 40% of a surface sample will pass through a 2-mm sieve, the receptive stage has been reached and pioneer species begin to germinate and grow into mature plants.

Frequently the weathering process moves rapidly to the point where the surface of the heap is covered with a layer of hard irregularly-shaped plates possessing high resistance to further breakdown. When this occurs, as mentioned previously, the effect of wind and rain is to remove such fine material as becomes detached, so that the surface may remain incapable of supporting plant growth for many years. The opposite property, that of having an excess of easily weathered shale and clay, may also develop; here the surface is quickly reduced to uniform particle size, and it has a tendency to become impervious under conditions of high rainfall. This in itself discourages plant growth but, coupled with cracking and low moisture content in the summer months, the total effect is one which may prevent or greatly retard the establishment of vegetation. Clearly, a great deal will depend upon the rates of the following three processes:

(a) disintegration of the spoil material,
(b) removal of the fine particles by run-off of rain water or by wind,
(c) spread of the successful plant colonists.

Wherever (b) greatly exceeds (a), the chances are small that a vegetative cover will be able to form. Those plants that can exploit the situation where (a) and (b) are almost equal might provide the initial members of a successful plant association. The natural establishment of vegetation is a hazardous process.

(2) *The oxidation of bituminous matter leading to the burning of spoil*

heaps. When bituminous material is exposed to the air in spoil heaps, slow oxidation commences and, if the heat of reaction liberated during the process is unable to escape rapidly enough, some parts of the heap may be raised to the ignition temperature. Heaps of mixed sizes appear to be more likely to heat than uniformly fine material. This is because the larger pieces tend to keep the texture open and permit sufficient ventilation for oxidation, and hence heating, to proceed.

The physical condition of the waste, as well as the methods of tipping, will determine the amount of shattering it undergoes, and hence these are also factors affecting the rate of oxidation. Very brittle waste of high carbon content, tipped with equal amounts of hard argillaceous spoil, will provide large surface areas for oxidation, together with an open texture to facilitate ventilation. The modern view is that a high pyrites (FeS_2) content will not itself promote spontaneous heating in pit heaps. Nevertheless, the weathering of the 'brasses' (FeS_2), and the subsequent breakdown of the bituminous material in which they are embedded, will produce fresh oxidizable surfaces; in addition, there is also the appreciable amount of heat evolved in the oxidation of the pyrites.

The presence of a high sulphur content will play some part in the heating process. In an open-textured heap, ventilation is improved with increasing temperature, and the fire spreads rapidly throughout the mass. Many burning tips give off a great deal of smoke and fumes having a distinct bituminous smell, while others give off strong sulphurous fumes.

In some heaps, a sublimate rich in sulphur of high purity and also containing ammonium chloride is deposited on the shales around the holes through which the gases escape. Analysis of the shales around the vents reveals the presence of alums compounded from the sulphates of ammonia and potassium, and the sulphates of aluminium and ferric-iron.

Under the action of heat the coaly material is burnt to an ash with the evolution of carbon dioxide and water, and the pyritic sulphur is partly evolved in the form of sulphur according to the equation

$$FeS_2 = FeS + S$$

The ferrous sulphide then may either undergo oxidation or recombination. In the presence of ample oxygen supplies, oxidation may proceed as in this equation:

$$4FeS + 7O_2 = 2Fe_2O_3 + 4SO_2$$

The other possibility is the combination of the ferrous sulphide with other constituents of the ash to form ferrous silicate with the liberation of sulphur. This process is thought to assist the formation of clinker, as ferrous silicates have a low melting-point. It is believed that one fraction of the sulphur is distilled off as vapour, another condensed on the surface of the heap, and a third converted to sulphuric acid.

Another effect of the intense heat (temperatures of 500 °C are quite common) generated in a burning heap is to fracture and split the large shales by decomposing the jointing materials. This may leave the surface of the heap covered with characteristic brick-red-coloured layers of small platy shales. Where the shales are softer and of higher coal-content, burning may leave a light brown or apricot-coloured material which rapidly weathers to a fine smooth powder.

(3) *Acid conditions at the surface of spoil heaps.* Even the purest form of coal leaves a residue of ash after normal combustion; the ash represents the mineral matter present in the plants which gave rise to the coal-peat. A fraction of the ash is made up of sulphur, which is present in coal measure rocks in three forms: as organic sulphur, as pyrites or marcasite (substances that are similar chemically but differ in crystalline form and ease of oxidation) or as sulphates. It is thought that the pyrites was introduced into the coal measures either by bacterial activity during the peat stage, or later in solution of iron sulphate subsequent to the formation of the coal. The iron pyrites may be in particles disseminated throughout the mass, or confined to the clay minerals in the joints. The total sulphur content present in colliery spoil can vary from a trace to over 12% and, because spoil is composed of a mixture of waste coal, shaley coal, shale, seggar clay and stone, the total sulphur content varies from one district to another, and even from heap to heap.

Iron pyrites at or near the surface of a shale heap comes in contact with air and water, and chemical reactions such as the following may occur. First the oxidation produces ferrous sulphate and sulphuric acid:

(i) $2FeS_2 + 7O_2 + 2H_2O = 2FeSO_4 + 2H_2SO_4$

Further oxidation is retarded in the presence of sulphuric acid, so that ferrous sulphate and sulphuric acid may be leached out of the heap together. It is supposed that in time the acid concentration is reduced by dilution to a point where further oxidation can occur. This results in the formation of ferric sulphate.

(ii) $4FeSO_4 + O_2 + 2H_2SO_4 = 2Fe_2(SO_4)_3 + 2H_2O$

Finally, when the acid concentration is sufficiently reduced by rainfall, the ferric sulphate hydrolyzes to give sulphuric acid and ferric hydroxide. This compound causes the characteristic rusty colour of the water draining from some of our larger spoil heaps. Thus all the sulphur bound with iron in insoluble pyrites can appear in the drainage as sulphuric acid.

(iii) $$Fe_2(SO_4)_3 + 6H_2O = 2Fe(OH)_3 + 3H_2SO_4$$

The sulphuric acid attacks the shales, liberating the bases, chiefly aluminium, iron and potassium, and converting these into sulphates.

There is evidence also that the formation of sulphuric acid from coal measure rocks may be caused, at least in part, by the action of micro-organisms as well as by atmospheric oxidation.

Whatever the mechanism of acid formation, the moist oxidation of sulphur-bearing rocks of the coal measures appears to result in the appearance of free sulphuric acid, and this lowers the pH to values lethal to living plants. There are several factors which bear on the rate of oxidation of iron sulphide. The proportion of pyrites to marcasite will be important, because the latter oxidizes much more readily than pyrites. The rate of weathering of the material in which the pyrites is embedded or dispersed is important, for on this depends the speed with which the surfaces of the sulphide mineral can be exposed to atmospheric agents. Experiments show that the rate of oxidation is increased by the degree of fineness of the mineral, and by an increase in temperature. When exposed to moist air, marcasite particularly becomes covered with an efflorescence of ferrous sulphate; the rate of removal of this layer by washing with rain water will control the progress of further oxidation.

The rate of colonization of spoil heaps containing sulphur-bearing rocks will clearly be influenced by all the above processes and the conditions resulting from them. The position of balance between the rate of formation of sulphuric acid and sulphates on the one hand, and the rate at which these products are leached out of the surface layers on the other, may determine whether or not vegetation can succeed. Some seeds may be able to germinate on ground with a high sulphur content, and then the degree of acidity will largely govern those that can survive.

Where a pit heap has taken fire and burnt out, one can expect to find present in the upper layers, for a short time after cooling, the products of the oxidation of pyrites, i.e. ferric oxide, ferric sulphate, sulphuric acid and elemental sulphur. Generally the sulphuric acid will leach out quickly, or it may react with the bases in the shales to form sulphates, which leach out more slowly. The double possibility exists that: (a) acid sulphates may be formed and remain in the upper layers for a short time, and (b) where there was an appreciable sulphur content before combustion, the surface layers could easily remain acid for a time. Gradually as leaching proceeds, the pH rises until the surface has lost all its acid. This position is distinct from that on an unburnt pit heap containing pyritiferous waste where, due to local rates of weathering and leaching, the surface may remain at high acidity for a long period, during which plant growth cannot occur or is severely retarded. This effect may be due jointly to the low pH-values, and to the presence of toxic substances released more readily into acidic solution.

In reclamation work, acidity can be reduced by working ground limestone into the surface layers, and up to 10 tons/acre (25,000 kg/ha) may be required to raise the soil reaction to pH 7. However, not all sites respond favourably when lime is used to reduce the acidity and, contrary to expectations, there may be reduced growth as the neutral point (pH 7) is approached. Care must be taken to perform tests to find the exact lime requirement. Furthermore, there is the danger that added lime may form an impervious crust at the surface if it reacts with soil compounds. When it is not feasible to carry out liming, one alternative is to accelerate leaching by means of a fine water spray, or using the normal rainfall and a surface mulch. Another method is to plant a selection of acid-tolerant species.

High surface temperatures
Temperature is one of the important factors that control the individual processes and reactions in living plants. The rate of growth and the form it takes is the resultant effect of temperature on all of the separate processes of photosynthesis, transpiration, respiration, flower formation, etc. All the metabolic processes that lead to growth depend upon the existence in plant cells of a healthy protoplasm; because protoplasmic activity is substantially affected by changes in temperature, it is clear that at every stage in the life cycle of plants, from the inhibition of water by the seed prior to germination through the processes of growth and development to the ripening of the seed, temperature can be a controlling influence. It is the soil temperature that first affects plant growth by its action during germination.

Soil temperature is largely dependent on solar radiation, and one factor which influences the amount of absorption of the incident radiation is soil colour. Black surfaces have higher absorptive powers than light-coloured ones, and it is also true that a surface which is a good absorber is a good radiator and a poor reflector. Therefore, it is not surprising to find that in sunlight the surface temperatures of black shale are greater than those of cream/yellow Magnesian Limestone (Table 3.1).

In the northern hemisphere, temperatures on south-facing slopes are higher than those on north slopes; this is because the amount of radiation per unit area reaching the surface is proportional to the cosine of the angle (θ) between the direction of the sun's rays and a perpendicular to the surface. Because the slopes on pit heaps are often between 30° and

Table 3.1 Temperatures taken simultaneously at the surface of comparable adjacent plots on Magnesian Limestone and colliery spoil heaps.

Time of day (hours)	Temperature (°C)	
	Limestone	Shale
1100	20·5	23·5
1200	24·0	30·0
1300	28·5	37·0
1400	38·0	53·0
1500	39·0	53·5
1600	38·0	53·0
1700	34·0	45·0

43°, there are times when the sun's rays are at right angles to the surface on south slopes (i.e. $\theta = 0$ and $\cos \theta = 1$) and at grazing angle on north slopes (i.e. $\theta = 89°$ and $\cos \theta = 0·02$).

It has been calculated that on pit heaps the south slopes may receive about ten times the energy falling on north slopes, and consequently are much warmer. The temperature difference is reflected in the results of seeding experiments carried out in the spring and autumn on moist slopes. South slopes have a distinct advantage for early emergence and good growth. In summer, however, the combination of slope, aspect and colour of pit heaps produces conditions which result in very high temperatures over long periods—far above the lethal temperatures for young roots and shoots. Protoplasm only functions normally up to certain temperatures, and thereafter damage leading to death occurs. For example, with some 6-week-old seedlings of *Picea abies* (Norway spruce) rooted in moist soil, after a treatment at 45 °C for 6 h, the mortality was 3%, whereas at 65 °C for the same time the death rate increased twenty times. It is not uncommon to find temperatures of over 50 °C (with the maximum over 60 °C) at the surface of pit heaps for up to six hours daily in summer; this leads to heat injury and to the death of germinating seedlings.

Surface temperatures of 50 °C and more have been recorded on dry black shale as soon as one day following rain and when the air temperature above the surface was only 25 °C. Seven days after rain as the surface lost nearly all its moisture the temperatures approached 70 °C. The highest surface temperature ever recorded on black colliery spoil seems to be 80 °C; the air temperature at the time was 45 °C.

The temperatures at points beneath the surface are determined by the thermal properties of the spoil materials. Because shaley material has a higher specific heat than organic material, the rate of heat transfer downwards from the surface is greater in disintegrated raw shale than in the young soil that is formed from it as plant colonists add organic matter to the surface. The thermal conductivity of water is about 30 times that of the air it displaces in a soil. In a dry loam soil we would therefore expect to find less heat conducted down into the heap than in a moist mineral one where the lower levels warm up more rapidly. In tests on a dry shaley soil, when the surface temperature was 50 °C, the temperature at 3 in (7·6 cm) was 33 °C, at 6 in (15·2 cm) 25 °C, and at 9 in (22·9 cm) 21 °C. The slopes of pit heaps where these high surface temperatures were recorded were generally south-facing and supported little or no vegetation. It could be argued that germinating seedlings and young plants died because of injury, such as heat girdling of the shoot at the surface of the spoil and by leaf scorching. However, a more likely explanation for the failure of seedlings to become established is based on the harmful combined effects of temperature and drought; this is discussed below.

It has long been known that an organic or mineral mulch, or a plant cover, reduces considerably the maximum temperature and the range of fluctuations in the ground beneath. Extracts from temperature records which were taken in July/August at points on a spoil heap where there was (a) bare ground, (b) a moss-lichen layer (1·5 cm thick) and (c) closed swards of *Agrostis tenuis* (common bent grass) and (d) *Holcus mollis* (creeping soft grass) are given in Table 3.2

Table 3.2   Temperatures in the surface layers of bare or colonized places on a pit heap.

A. surface temperature ranges	
(i) Bare ground	8 to 50 °C = 42 °C
(ii) Moss-lichen mat	9 to 52 °C = 43 °C
(iii) *Agrostis* sward	13 to 26 °C = 13 °C
(iv) *Holcus* sward	11 to 20 °C = 9 °C
B. temperatures at 3 in (7·6 cm) underground	
(i) Bare ground	11 to 34 °C = 23 °C
(ii) Moss-lichen mat	12 to 29 °C = 17 °C
(iii) *Agrostis* sward	15 to 19 °C = 4 °C
(iv) *Holcus* sward	15 to 16 °C = 1 °C

The insulating properties of a grass sward, and particularly of a thin layer of moss and lichen, are well demonstrated. It seems that even a thin layer of vegetation so reduces the effect of high temperatures that roots of seedlings and rhizomes of established plants are not subjected to temperatures higher than about 30 °C. Furthermore, after rain the vegetation protects the layers beneath it from evaporation losses, and this also produces conditions that favour the growth of plants.

Figure 3.1*a* A typical pit heap.

Available water supply

The analysis of heat conduction in soils in the field is complex because the surface is exposed seasonally, daily and even hourly to changes of radiation, and also because there are similar changes in soil water content. In general, periods of high soil temperature coincide with periods of low moisture content. Under these conditions, water loss from plants may exceed supply, and a negative water balance results.

The creation of water deficits on balance is due, not to stoppage of supply, but to an insufficiently rapid supply. Thus they may be brought about (*a*) by the promotion of transpiration (water loss from leaves) through the opening of stomatal apertures, the drying of the air, or the rising of the wind; or (*b*) by the retarding of absorption and conduction through the drying of the soil, or the reduction of temperature.

Plants which lack water may wilt. We associate wilting in the summer with periods of drought and with soils which lack available water. Soils are sometimes said to be physically wet but physiologically dry, because it has been found that the percentage of water that a soil must contain to save plants from wilting depends upon the nature of the soil. Thus the permanent wilting-point (i.e. the water content of a soil, expressed as a percentage of its dry weight, when irreversible wilting occurs) might fluctuate for a given plant from less than 2% for a sand to 18% for a clay loam. At wilting-point, water is held by the soil with great tenacity compared with the water-retaining forces acting at field capacity. (While *permanent wilting-point* (PWP) is the lower limit of water content for plant growth, the upper is called the *field capacity*, and it is the amount of water held in the fine capillaries of a soil after rainfall when all drainage has ceased.) The water held between field capacity and wilting point is regarded as available for plant growth. For the surface layers of the spoil heap described below, the field capacity was 13% and PWP was 5%.

Weekly records of the moisture content were made throughout the year on a conical pit heap at the surface and at various depths, and at four different aspects (see Table 3.3). It was found that at the surface 66% of the moisture content values were below the permanent wilting point, and there was no significant difference between aspects (see Table 3.3).

Table 3.3 Percentage of the 55 weekly measurements of moisture content which were less than permanent wilting point.

Aspect	Surface	1 in	3 in	5 in
SW	69	53	25	19
SE	63	48	37	30
NE	64	44	15	6
NW	65	46	17	13

However, at 3 in (7·6 cm) there was a fall to 37% and 25% on the south-east and south-west, and to 17% and 15% on the north-west and north-east aspects. At 10 in (25·4 cm) the moisture content on all aspects remained constant at about the field capacity. These results reflected the distribution of plants on the heap, where the south, south-east and south-west remained bare of plants, while the northern slope supported a healthy mixed plant community.

These observations underline the possible importance of the rate of elongation of the roots of seedlings with respect to the progressive drying out from the soil surface downwards. Only so long as the extremities of the elongating root systems keep ahead of the downward extension of the dry zone will the plants be able to extract the water they require. From Table 3.3 it appears that even in dry weather the moisture contents at depths of 5 in (13 cm) rarely fall below PWP.

In some experiments to examine the effects of temperature and moisture content on survival of seedlings of the grasses *Agrostis tenuis* and *Dactylis glomerata* (cocksfoot), sowings were made in deep trays of fine shale sprayed with water to keep the moisture content at about 80% of field capacity (FC). After 5 weeks, electric lamps were arranged to maintain the soil surface temperature at 57 °C for 4 hours daily. Some trays remained about FC (12% moisture) while in others the surface layer had been allowed to fall to PWP (5% moisture).

Four fifths of the plants survived when there was an adequate supply

Figure 3.1*b* Trees on bare pit heap after 7 years of growth.

of available water, compared with about one tenth when there was little or none (see Table 3.4). For 20-week-old plants treated in the same way, the survival figures for the drier soil were 68% for *Agrostis* and 73% for *Dactylis*.

Table 3.4 Survival of 5-week-old grass seedlings at two differ-ent soil moisture contents when the soil surface temperature was 57 °C

Species	Soil water content	% Survival
Agrostis tenuis	5%	10%
	12%	85%
Dactylis glomerata	5%	11%
	13%	82%

These results can be related to events taking place in the field. Grass seeds ripen and are scattered by the wind in September and October. Assuming that they germinate within a few weeks and the young plants survive the winter frosts, their ages will be in the region of 24 weeks when they are subjected to the hot dry conditions of summer. Some seeds may remain dormant during the winter and then germinate in March or April. The seedlings will be about 6 weeks old when drought conditions have to be faced. Thus, it appears that, in the field, many plants that are

6 weeks old could survive the summer provided the moisture content of the soil remained near to FC (12%). If drying out occurs due to the absence of rainfall, so that the moisture content falls to PWP (5%), the percentage of surviving plants would be small. On the other hand, many of the plants that are 24 weeks old at the beginning of the summer could survive, even when the soil moisture content falls to the PWP or below.

It has been argued that the cooling effect of transpiration may save certain plants growing in the open from injury. The effectiveness of transpiration in transferring energy from a leaf to the atmosphere is demonstrated by the following example. In an experiment, the rate of transpiration was 5×10^{-4} g/cm^2 per minute, and the latent heat of vaporization of water was taken as 585 calories per gram (cal/g). This gives an energy loss $(0.5 \times 10^{-3} \times 5.85 \times 10^2)$ cal, i.e. 0.3 cal $(1.2$ J$)$, and this was sufficient to lower the temperature of a freely transpiring plant by 15 °C. In experiments in growth rooms with well-watered mesophytic plants, the temperature of the air was raised in steps from 10 to 60 °C. For air temperatures below about 30 °C, leaves were warmer, but above 30 °C cooler, than their surroundings. This contrasting behaviour of leaves was closely examined at higher temperatures. Just below 41.5 °C the rate of transpiration was 5×10^{-4} g/cm^2 per minute. However, at 41.5 °C the rate increased rapidly to 22×10^{-4} g/cm^2 per minute. The additional cooling effect was sufficient to prevent leaf temperatures from exceeding 42 °C, even when the air temperature was raised to 60 °C. It was concluded that abundant water supply which allowed rapid transpiration accounted for the low leaf temperature.

Plant nutrients

For healthy growth to occur, plants must have a supply of essential mineral elements; some of them, the macronutrients, are required in relatively large amounts and others, the trace elements, are required only in minute amounts (e.g. one part per hundred million of solution). All of these elements, which remain behind as ash when the organic material of the plant is burnt away, are taken up by the plant roots from the soil. There are seven recognized inorganic macronutrients, of which nitrogen (N), phosphorus (P) and potassium (K) are well known for their great influence on plant growth.

The parts played by the different elements in the life of plants have been identified, but it is worth noting that very little is known which would account for the importance to plants of potassium. Colliery shale usually contains potassium in amounts (100 ppm) comparable with those found in the plough layer of some arable soils. However, the content of nitrogen (e.g. 0 to 1 ppm) and phosphorus (e.g. trace to 10 ppm) in some shales is far

Figure 3.1c   Trees on bare pit heaps after 20 years.

below agricultural values, where 20 ppm N and P would be satisfactory. Because of the low initial N and P content, it is unlikely that natural colonization would succeed without the impetus provided by the activities of rabbits, hares and birds. The wide open spaces of many spoil heaps have a strong attraction for these creatures and, long before vegetation appears after the final tipping of waste, they are active on the heaps. Their trial burrows and resting places cause sufficient compaction of the spoil to form a seed-bed in which seeds can germinate and grow into mature flowering plants.

Equally important is the increase in the nitrogen content of the soil brought about by microbial action on the animal's droppings and on the dead remains of leaves, roots and stems. This organic litter is the source of food and energy of soil micro-organisms and, in the course of their life cycles, they gradually release nutrients locked up in the litter back to the soil in a form suitable for absorption by roots. Thus the nutrients are recycled, and at the same time the residual organic matter, which is traditionally associated with fertility, plays its part in improving the properties of the soil.

On bare shale, dressings of N and P fertilizers have a dramatic effect on plant growth. In some greenhouse experiments with grasses, when ammonium nitrate was used to give N at the rate of 100 lb/acre (112 kg/ha), the dry weight was three times that of the control; with added superphosphate of lime to give P at the rate of 45 lb/ac

(49 kg/ha), the yield was only slightly better than the control but, with addition of both N and P together, the yield was over six times the control. In another experiment the addition of N and P at the same rates gave a twenty-fold increase in yield. With tree seedlings, after one season the average height of controls was 2·4 in (6 cm) with added N 3·5 in (9 cm), with P 5·1 in (13 cm) and with N and P together trees were 14·2 in (36 cm) tall.

When vegetation is to be established on spoil heaps, it is important to determine the status of the available nutrients in the soil in order that the most suitable fertilizer may be selected. There is some evidence that tests commonly used for this purpose on agricultural soils may not produce accurate results when used on pit-heap waste. However, if the results of soil tests are taken as a basis for plant growth trials carried out in the field, a proper fertilizer treatment should emerge.

It is important in preparing colliery spoil heaps for planting to understand that each site is, in some respects, a special case and that there are disadvantages in extrapolating research results from one site to another. Where the objective is the growth of a herbaceous cover crop for amenity and site protection, the application of N and P and K each at the rate of 45 lb/acre (50 kg/ha) may be adequate. However, for other purposes, and on other sites, the rate of one or more of the fertilizer components may have to be raised many times before a crop can be supported.

In the early stages of soil formation on shale heaps, while organic matter is being incorporated with the mineral fraction to form a reasonable soil structure, the applied nitrogen is quickly lost from the top layers by leaching; the applied phosphorus often becomes just as rapidly converted into insoluble compounds and is therefore unavailable to plants. It is therefore important in the immediate post-reclamation years to monitor the site by means of soil tests and observations of the condition of the vegetation, and to add more fertilizer to meet any deficiency that occurs.

Some of the soils developing on shales contain adequate supplies of potassium, and it is argued that compound fertilizers (e.g. NPK, 20–15–15)* contain ions that are unnecessary for the fertilizing effect, and which may increase the osmotic pressure of the soil solution and adversely affect the growth of seedlings. For these conditions, use may be made of fertilizers containing only N and P. Seemingly a mixed fertilizer, such as ammonium nitrate and triple superphosphate of lime, is not as effective in providing balanced nutrition as one in which both N and P are present in the same granular substance. The compounds

* The figures indicate the percentages of N, P_2O_5 and K_2O.

Figure 3.1d   Reclaimed pit heap with grass and pines.

ammonium polyphosphate (15–61–0) and monoammonium phosphate (12–50–0) are said to be superior to urea ammonium phosphate (30–30–0) as an initial fertilizer applied to correct NP deficiencies.

Seed rate
After the spoil has been tipped, there follows a period during which the material settles down and undergoes a number of physical and chemical changes, some account of which has been given in the previous sections. Gradually the young surface soil improves in texture, so that in time it can hold water in sufficient quantities to maintain turgor in seedling plants developing in it. For non-toxic spoil, the receptive stage depends upon the conjunction in any one year of (*a*) suitable soil texture, (*b*) suitable amount of rainfall, and (*c*) suitable quantity of incoming seeds.

Up to a point it appears that a deficiency in one of these can be compensated by an excess in one or both of the other two. For example, a coarse-textured soil that would not normally retain sufficient water during the summer months to support young seedlings may in fact be able to do this if the rainfall is unusually high. Even if conditions return to normal in the following year, the chances are good that the young plants will be sufficiently well rooted to survive the summer drought.

The intensity of incoming seeds is critical because of the heavy losses which occur due to the high temperatures and drought, and to the open texture of the medium, which allows seeds to be carried to depths in the heap where germination and growth is impaired. It is an advantage for the seeds to enter the soil to some extent, for then protection against drying-out is given. Seeds that remain on the surface in the field rarely give rise to adult plants, because of the ease with which the delicate roots dry out and wither.

Experiments have shown that, although something of the order of 8×10^5 seeds per acre (3×10^6 seeds/ha) may be expected to arrive on the windward slopes of spoil heaps, only about one-seventh of them germinated and depending on the factors detailed above, only about one-twentieth of these survive to maturity. It was not surprising therefore to find that, when seeds of grasses were hand-sown on pit-heap slopes, the percentage survival was poor when the agricultural seed rate of $\frac{1}{12}$ oz/yd^2 (3 g/m^2) was used; not until rates of about 1 oz/yd^2 (34 g/m^2) were reached could a closed sward be confidently forecast in two years after planting.

These experiments suggest that even when the top layers of regraded spoil heaps are cultivated to produce a firm and slightly porous seed bed, compensation for the nature of the material should be made by raising the normal agricultural sowing rate.

Colonizing species

In north-east England the first plants to appear on spoil heaps to initiate the succession are generally grasses and herbs. There is no evidence that the algae, lichens, and mosses are usually amongst the early arrivals although, in isolated moist hollows on flat-topped heaps, they may sometimes appear in significant numbers. One reason for the virtual absence of these types may be that they are unable to survive on the dry platy shales that often form the soil surface in the pioneer stage. Nevertheless, when a closed cover of vegetation is developed, mosses do make their appearance in the community—but as a rule, they do not fill an important pioneer role.

Observations made at 250 sites in north-east England indicate the principal early colonists on spoil heaps (Table 3.5).

These naturally-occurring plant species can head a list of possible species that could be used in planting trials on colliery waste. But these early colonists give only a small clue to the choice of suitable species for planting. For example, there are plants found growing on pit heaps whose natural habitat is anything but a reliable guide to their usefulness in new surroundings. As an example of an unexpected pioneer plant, we can mention *Digitalis purpurea* (foxglove). Eleven specimens of the plant were found early in 1952 growing on the bare slopes of a spoil heap at Urpeth, County Durham; six of them flowered that season. *Digitalis* grew abundantly in the woodlands bordering the river Team one mile to the west of the spoil heaps. Bearing in mind the high seed production, the lightness of the seed and the direction of the prevailing wind, it seemed certain that the pit-heap colony had originated from seed blown eastwards from the Team Valley. The fact that this species can flourish on the spoil heaps points to its great ecological adaptability. The contrast between the woodland and the spoil heap habitats could hardly have been greater, for they differ in light intensity and temperature range, as well as in the extremes of chemical and physical composition. In spite of these differences, the colony grew in size and by 1956 no fewer than 250 plants grew at Urpeth.

Table 3.5 Principal early colonists on spoil heaps at 250 sites in N.E. England (The figures are the percentage of the sites where the species occur.)

(a) grasses: *Agrostis tenuis* (common bent) 82%
Dactylis glomerata (cocksfoot) 64%
Deschampsia flexuosa (wavy hair grass) 49%
Holcus lanatus (Yorkshire fog) 33%

(b) herbs: *Centaurea nigra* (lesser knapweed) 40%
Chamaenerion angustifolium (fireweed) 76%
Hieracium spp. (hawkweed), *H. pillosella* 68%
H. perpropinquum 80%
H. umbellatum 70%
Tussilago farfara (coltsfoot) 61%;

(c) shrubs: *Rosa* spp. (rose) 15%
Rubus sp. (bramble) 50%
Sarothamnus scoparius (broom) 17%
Ulex europaeus (whin) 12%

(d) trees: *Betula* (birch), (*B. pubescens*, *B. verrucosa*) 22%
Crataegus monogyna (hawthorn) 18%
Salix spp. (willow) 8%.

Similar successful growth on pit heaps has been achieved by *Deschampsia caespitosa* (tufted hair grass) and *Phalaris arundinacea* (reed grass), both described as damp-place plants, the former in woods and meadows, the latter in marshes, ponds and stream sides. Another plant of wet places is *Alnus glutinosa* (alder), which occurs in north-east England by stream sides and in low country. This plant is not listed above, nor has it ever been found growing naturally on pit heaps; and yet it is now recognized as being one of the most reliable species used in pit-heap reclamation. Similarly, *Trifolium repens* (white clover) is not listed as a frequent colonizing species, although it does occur naturally on a few spoil banks. Nevertheless, like *Alnus* it is an important part of seeds mixtures sown on regraded bare soil.

Reclamation methods

Earth works

A worked-out colliery site is made up of the heaps containing millions of tons of waste (some burnt to form hard clinkers and some unburnt), together with quantities of waste coal from the cleaning plant, and many derelict buildings. The engineering part of reclamation takes place first, and consists of the planned movement of the materials in such a way that the regraded site has rounded shapes and contours that convey to the observer an overall appearance of naturalness. In the course of moving the waste, steps should be taken to bury acid material (see p. 73), and clinker (see p. 71) beneath layers of less hostile material. Otherwise it could be more expensive to carry out the cultivation processes required to provide a medium in which grasses and trees can grow. The teeming of shales on to a pit heap from a tram or an overhead skip generally gives a loosely textured medium with a wide range of particle sizes, but in a reclamation site an impervious texture may occur. This is because earth-moving work is carried out with heavy-wheeled scrapers; these cause severe shearing and compaction as layer after layer of spoil is brought into place. There is evidence to show that better growth of plants is achieved where at least the last 4 feet of material is placed by tracked vehicles having ground contact pressure of $7\cdot3$ lb/in^2 ($0\cdot5$ kg/cm^2) instead of by wheeled scrapers with ten times the pressure.

Most schemes for growing grasses and trees on pit heaps are concerned with establishing a new soil from the shale material. To achieve this more quickly than by the natural processes described on p. 67, it is necessary to prepare the surface for sowing in the following ways:

(a) neutralize any acidity
(b) break up the shales so that there is a high proportion of particles in the 2–0·002 mm range
(c) build up the organic content
(d) develop soil structure.

This preparation is started before seed planting and it is continued afterwards. The incorporation of organic matter (e.g. sewage sludge, woollen waste, poultry manure, etc.) may take place towards the end of the seed-bed preparation, and the inorganic fertilizers may be added at the time of sowing the seeds. It is true that seeds can simply be broadcast on the site and left without further attention, but as we have seen (p. 79), losses are likely to be high both before and after germination. Therefore, some cultivation is helpful, but the amount will depend on, amongst other things, the purpose of the crop and the money available.

For amenity purposes the treatment may be slight compared with that given when an agricultural use is intended, and there will also be

differences between the preparations given on flat sites and on steep slopes.
The cultivations on a regraded heap may be summarized as follows:

(a) plough (including deep ripping if there is compaction).
(b) remove large stones.
(c) spread and incorporate lime.
(d) spread and incorporate organic material.
(e) harrow and roll.
(f) sow seeds, fertilizer and possibly a mulch.

Raw shale has no soil structure and, unlike a well-developed arable soil,
it is not resilient enough to withstand heavy machinery without being
compacted. The extent of this deformation increases with moisture
content and, even well below field capacity, severe compaction may occur.
It is a rule of farming to keep tillage implements off the land until it
dries out, and it is clearly important that this practice should be even
more closely followed in pit-heap reclamation.

There may be occasions when the spoil is too toxic to respond to
physical and chemical treatment in a reasonable time and at a reasonable
cost. If there is no supply of inert shale available to blanket the surface,
there may be a case for spreading topsoil. In each case, the cost of the
topsoiling must be carefully weighed against the cost of prolonged surface
treatment. Where a sufficient depth of topsoil can be used to cover the
site, much of the surface cultivations are at once eliminated, and so is
much of the maintenance that may be necessary in its absence.

Plants in reclamation
The second stage in the restoration of debased areas concerns the
planting of trees, grasses and herbs on the prepared ground in order that
the formation of a new soil may be initiated and fertility returned to
the land.

(i) *Grass seeds mixtures.* A grass-legume mixture is essential for establishing the initial continuous cover on regraded spoil in the shortest time.
Given a well-prepared seed bed and moist weather, a balanced seeds
mixture will in six weeks after sowing produce a sward that is so close
that from a distance of 20 yards none of the original surface is visible.
The choice of seeds is based on the criteria that were outlined on
pp. 69–82.

(a) resistance to drought and high temperature,
(b) tolerance of acid soil and little tilth,
(c) modest nutrient demands,
(d) well-developed root system,
(e) ability to quickly develop a ground cover,
(f) ability to stabilize the surface layers and initiate the formation of a new soil.

Plant growth is seasonal, and therefore no attempt should be made to sow seeds in a known dry period. This is important in horticultural and agricultural practice, and it is doubly important in pioneer shale soils. A large number of grasses have been tested for use in reclamation work in Great Britain, Europe and the United States, and the following have been found suitable:

Agrostis tenuis (common bent)
Agropyron cristatum (crested wheat)
Bromus inermis (smooth brome)
Dactylis glomerata (cocksfoot)
Festuca rubra (red fescue)
Festuca ovina (sheep's fescue)
Lolium perenne (perennial ryegrass)
Poa pratensis (Kentucky bluegrass).

A danger with some grasses is that they compete too strongly with young trees in their early stages of growth; if tree planting is to follow later, grasses like *Dactylis* and *Lolium* should be avoided.

Leguminous plants such as *Trifolium repens* (white clover), *Lotus corniculatus* (bird's foot trefoil), *Melilotus* spp. (sweet clover), *Coronilla varia* (crown vetch), etc., are important components of the seeds mixture because they can fix the nitrogen of the air by means of the bacteria which live symbiotically on their roots. These plants growing in a sward may fix up to 54 lb/acre (60 kg/ha) nitrogen per year, and hence make a valuable contribution to soil fertility. The inoculation of the seeds with specific strains of the bacteria *Rhizobium* may be needed on spoil where there is little or no bacterial population.

The rates and the times of fertilizer application needed to raise the nutrient level will vary from site to site. In some local conditions it was found necessary, as a result of soil tests, to apply large amounts of a phosphate fertilizer, e.g. 6 cwt/acre (750 kg/ha) superphosphate of lime, during the preparation of the seed bed, and then the NPK fertilization was carried out just before sowing. The NPK (20–15–15) was given at a rate of 4 cwt/acre (500 kg/ha), and this was followed by the same treatment each year for two years. A seeds mixture was sown at four times the agricultural rate, i.e. at 100 lb/acre (112 kg/ha) and it contained the following species:

Agrostis tenuis
Dactylis glomerata
Festuca rubra
F. ovina (tenuifolia)
Trifolium repens
T. pratense.

In some situations it is convenient to sow the seed broadcast, and in others the seed is drilled into position. With the latter method the advantage is that the seed is put into the ground at the required depth, in the right amount, and is immediately firmed in. Under conditions of steep slope, low bearing strength, or general inaccessibility, where conventional sowing cannot reasonably be carried out, hydroseeding is a useful alternative method. Here the selected seeds and fertilizers are mixed in a mobile tank with wood cellulose fibre, shredded sugar cane and water to form a pulp which is then sprayed under pressure on to the surface. The layer of organic mulch is about 0·25 in (0·6 cm) thick, and it protects the seeds from drying out during germination by conserving the water in the spoil and by insulating the seeds from high surface temperatures. Protection is also given against soil erosion, and against animal predators and high wind. The cellulose mantle acts as a food supply for soil micro-organisms, and it slowly disappears once the grass leaves emerge. The composition of a typical mulch used in hydroseeding may be as follows:

seeds 100 lb/acre (112 kg/ha)
fibre 2000 lb/acre (2240 kg/ha)
fertilizer 1000 lb/acre (1120 kg/ha).

Mulching may also be done with an inert material such as bitumen emulsion. The seed bed is prepared in the normal way; the seeds are sown and covered with a layer of sharp sand, and then the emulsion of bitumen and water is sprayed on top. Finally, the emulsion film is covered with a thin layer of sand. According to the dilution, the emulsion penetrates below the surface and holds the seeds in a moist microclimate favouring quick germination. To add organic matter to the soil at germination, a mulch of chopped straw may be spread over the surface after sowing, and then the bitumen is sprayed over the mulch. Alternatively, seeds and fertilizers can be mixed with water, sprayed on the raw spoil, and then a mulch of wood cellulose fibre and bitumen emulsion is sprayed over the seeded surface. Finally, surface protection may also be afforded by rolls of jute matting laid out on the shale after seed sowing is completed. Aerial seeding, which is applicable in some aspects of derelict land and reclamation, does not seem to be relevant to deep coal mine spoil. Seeds and fertilizers are dropped on to the unprepared surface where the losses are usually very high.

Grasses and herbs can also be established on spoil heaps in the form of turves. Turf laying is an expensive operation which would normally be applied to large areas, but it could be worth while on a small scale to deal with special site conditions such as slopes subject to erosion. The turves must be taken with as deep a cut as possible to avoid severe root pruning, and they must contain grasses and herbs likely to succeed on spoil banks. Commercially available turves, by virtue of their thickness and species content, are not likely to be suitable for exposed slopes. The shale must be well broken up in the planting hole. Organic matter and slow-acting fertilizers must be added to encourage root growth. The turves are planted level with the surrounding shale, and the site watered until they become established. The turves, which may require to be pegged down, should not be planted in unbroken lines but instead have gaps between every two or three to allow for run-off.

(ii) *Trees and shrubs.* Tree planting on spoil heaps in Britain has a long history, and for about 150 years it has been carried out sporadically. Some early plantations were made in the 1820s by the Earl of Dudley at places in Staffordshire; in the 1830s by the Earl of Durham at Chester-le-Street; and thereafter by single individuals and by groups, such as the Midland Reafforestation Association (1903) and the South-West Durham Improvement Association (1927), and by others in most of the coalfields. Their common aim was "to beautify, and, at the same time, to utilize the unsightly refuse heaps which are left on the closing down of collieries".

Near the tops of high spoil heaps, where exposure to sun and wind is greatest, the transpiration stress is high and a well-developed root system is required to maintain an adequate water supply to growing shoots. Negative water balances will frequently develop by the end of a dry windy day, and these must be eliminated at night when stomatal transpiration is minimal. Prolonged water deficits lead to loss of turgor, and permanent damage to growing points. Long experience with growing trees on poor soils in exposed places led early planters to favour conifers rather than native broad-leaved trees, and the following have been successful in a wide range of sites in Britain and elsewhere:

Pinus contorta (lodgepole pine)
P. murgo (mountain pine)
P. nigra var. austriaca (Austrian pine)
P. nigra var. calabrica (Corsican pine)
P. sylvestris (Scots pine)
Pices abies (Norway spruce)
P. sitchensis (Sitka spruce)
Larix decidua (European larch)
L. leptolepis (Japanese larch).

In the north-east of England the conifers *P. contorta* and *P. nigra* var. *calabrica* were very successful on spoil heaps. Both species made only modest increments of height 0·08 m (3 in) per year for the first seven or eight years but after 10 years the annual increase rose by over six times and after 15 years by eight times to 0·64 m (25 in). The trees growing on exposed tops of heaps averaged 1·5 m (5 ft) after 10 years' growth compared with those on the lower slopes where the average height was 3·0 m (10 ft).

As could be forecast from knowledge of the drying power of the prevailing south-west wind, the east slopes favoured growth in the early stages, but after 20 years the trees do equally well on all aspects, and only slightly less well on the tops. There is no record of conifers growing naturally on spoil heaps in north-east England as do the broad-leaved trees. Of these *Betula* spp. *B. pubescens*, *B. verrucosa* (birch) is the earliest colonist, and it was present on a quarter of 250 sites examined.

Birches seem to thrive on the large bare surfaces of pit heaps, where the relatively high temperatures and light intensities favour germination and early growth. Furthermore, the roots penetrate deep into the spoil, and there is a good balance between root and shoot to give resistance against drought. Birch has high acid tolerance, and experiments show the growth rate is hardly affected within the pH range 3·5 to 8·0. It has low requirement for phosphate, but it needs higher nitrogen. Birch seeds tend to germinate where tufts of grass have created tiny platforms on which organic matter accumulates, and the implication is that the nitrogen requirement may be supplied from this source. It has been said that birch is difficult to plant on pit-heap material, and instances of high failure rates have been advanced in support of its unsuitability. But its outstanding success as a natural colonist encouraged some further investigation, and it now seems that the fault lies with bad planting methods and not with the tree itself. Correctly planted trees reached a height of nearly 33 ft (10 m) in 20 years.

Unlike *Betula* spp., *Alnus glutinosa* was not found as a natural colonist on any of the 250 sites examined. It is a wet-place plant, normally found by lakes and streams, and in a woodland succession to marsh and fen. However, it is clearly very well suited to spoil heaps, where it grows at about the same rate as *Betula*; because it does not suffer any check on transplanting, after 5 years it is usually the tallest pioneer tree. The common explanation of this success is that *Alnus* has nitrogen-fixing abilities and a high rate of root growth. Although *Alnus* is said to be short-lived in certain poor soils, there is no evidence of this on colliery spoil, and it remains the best broad-leaved tree to start a plantation. In the past, *Robinia pseudoacacia* (black locust) has been another nitrogen-fixing species used for pioneer planting on spoil heaps. It grows rapidly and forms crown closure at an early age. It is tolerant of acid spoil, and in 20 years it may grow to a height of 12 m (39 ft). So far as other hardwoods are concerned, field trials show that *Acer pseudoplatanus* (sycamore), *Crataegus monogyna* (hawthorn), *Fagus sylvatica* (beech), *Fraxinus excelsior* (ash), *Prunus avium* (wild cherry), *Quercus* spp. (oak), *Sorbus aucuparia* (rowan), *S. aria* (whitebeam) do not make good pioneer trees, and they should only be planted in colliery spoil after a high level of fertility has been attained. For example, out of a total of over 21,000 *Acer pseudoplatanus* (sycamore) planted on bare spoil heaps, only a few hundred survived in a stunted form after 20 years. In contrast, on many low mounds of spoil where the vegetation has been slowly passing through a succession for over a hundred years (see p. 63), where the organic content is now 10%, the pH 5·8 and the nitrogen content 200 ppm, tall sycamore trees are the dominant species.

Trees planted on the barren slopes of spoil heaps will do nothing for many years to control erosion or to improve the colour (see illustrations). Bearing in mind the low initial level of fertility in pit-heap soil, it is not surprising that tree planting made directly into shale often results in poor growth and trees suffer high losses. However, when grasses and herbs are established and a fertile top layer has begun to develop, selected trees do extremely well on pit heap spoil, either in the place it was tipped or in regraded spoil. A grass sward enhances tree growth, because there is increased microbial activity in the soil; erosion is reduced, and insulation is provided against high surface temperature. It is a wise precaution therefore to sow grasses first, taking care to eliminate those grasses such as *Lolium perenne* that compete strongly against trees in their early years and to favour less-demanding species such as *Agrostis tenuis* (see p. 85).

In the past, loam and fertilizers have often been placed in the planting hole; this has encouraged root growth without in any way restricting the outward spread of roots. To avoid difficulties of transport, the roots surrounded by soil can be contained in a hessian bag tied at the neck. Trees may be pruned to give a good balance between shoot and roots, and to prevent excessive movement in the wind (which snaps roots and strips bark from young trees at ground level). In tree planting on pit heaps it has never been considered worth while to do anything in the way of staking or other protection from the wind, and the difficulty has been met by a higher rate of planting than normal; even if some trees perish, there will be sufficient left, and thinning out may be done later if necessary.

Conclusion

All the signs suggest that in many countries coal mining will continue to be one of the chief causes of derelict land. In future the waste material will be disposed of more carefully than in the past. Some may be tipped at sea, back filled, or used in civil engineering, but most will be progressively reclaimed for agriculture, recreation and building purposes. Large areas of abandoned tips and colliery sites remain to be improved.

From past research, the difficulties of turning pit heaps into pastures are fairly well understood, and there are several completed reclamation schemes as evidence that satisfactory techniques have been worked out. Some enlightened local authorities have already decided that this is the right time to take advantage of modern methods of blending spoil heaps into the landscape and making them support vegetation.

FURTHER READING

General texts

Robert Arvill (1969), *Man and Environment*, Pelican Books.
John Barr (1969), *Derelict Britain*, Pelican Books, Harmondsworth, Middlesex, England.
R. O. Whyte and J. W. B. Sisam (1949), *The Establishment of Vegetation on Industrial Waste Land*, Commonwealth Agricultural Bureaux, Aberystwyth.

More specialized texts

Tony Aldous (1972), *Battle for the Environment*, Collins, Glasgow.
Ed. M. J. Chadwick and G. T. Goodman (1975), *The Ecology of Resource Degradation and Renewal*, Blackwell, Oxford.
Ed. R. J. Hutnik and G. M. Davis (1973), *Ecology and Reclamation of Devastated Land*, Vol. 1 and 2, Gordon and Breach, London.
Ed. G. T. Goodman, R. W. Edwards and J. M. Lambert (1965), *Ecology and the Industrial Society*, Blackwell, Oxford.
Landscape Reclamation, Vol. 1 1971, Vol. 2 1972, I.P.C. Science and Technology Press, Guildford.

CHAPTER FOUR

LAND IMPROVEMENT IN THE HILLS AND UPLANDS OF SCOTLAND

JOHN B. McCREATH

THIS CHAPTER IS DIVIDED INTO TWO SECTIONS. THE FIRST DEALS WITH THE general scientific and economic principles of land improvement in the hills and uplands, with special reference to hill sheep farming; the second gives a detailed consideration of a weed problem (bracken) which is of particular significance to this sector of the agricultural industry.

Introduction

Within the physical framework of the land and its associated climate, the farming pattern of any country has been shaped by the skill and energy of successive generations responding to economic realities. Seen from the watch-tower of history, the process is not static, nor is it always a smooth upward progression. Much of the arable low ground, taken for granted today, had to be carved out in earlier times. In the hill and upland areas, in times of prosperity, the "low-ground frontier" is pushed higher up the hill; in periods of depression, the frontier recedes as the improved land reverts to its original state. Owing to climate and relief, the hills represent the greatest challenge to improvement within the limits of economic feasibility. Whereas the physical factors are to a large degree basic and unchanging, economic factors can and do alter rapidly over time; but the possible response to change is conditioned by the rigidity of the physical framework. This applies to agriculture generally, and very markedly to hill farming.

Climate

For any form of agriculture, the two fundamental factors are climate and soil; in hill country, altitude and topography are of special significance. Scotland lies within the latitude range of 54° and 61°N. Fortunately, due to the influence of the Gulf Stream Drift off the western seaboard and to the predominantly south-westerly air flow carrying a large importation of heat from the equatorial regions, the climate is in marked contrast to that of continental regions at the same latitude: compare, for example, Glasgow and Moscow. At lower elevations, the general picture is one of mild winters and summers as cool as any in Europe. The penalty—small in relation to the benefits of this oceanic influence—is higher rainfall. Another feature of Scotland's weather is windiness, particularly in the north-west. For such a small country, the variability of the weather from day to day, and between districts on the same day, is unique.

On the hills and uplands, the altitude effect means more precipitation, often in the form of snow. Over a wide area of the western and more mountainous side of the country, the mean annual rainfall is well in excess of 60 inches (1500 mm), rising to over 100 inches (2500 mm) on the hill tops, whereas on the eastern side, some upland areas have less than 45 inches (1125 mm). Wind speed increases with altitude; the combined effect of wind and rain imposes considerable stress on livestock, to the extent that only hardy breeds of hill sheep and hill cattle can be outwintered— the latter only if there is some natural shelter. Sustained high winds also have a detrimental effect on plant growth, and this limitation, peculiar to Britain and particularly to Scotland, is becoming increasingly recognized. The greater degree of cloud cover means less global radiation and lower temperatures than in lowland areas. Mean temperature decreases with height by 1 °F per 300 feet (1 °C per 165 m).

Adopting the conventional threshold temperature (42 °F = 5·6 °C) at which temperate plants begin actively to grow, it is clear that the onset of "spring" growth will be delayed, and the length of the growing season shortened as altitude increases. Evidence from the meteorological observatory at Eskdalemuir in the Southern Uplands indicates a decrease of 10 days for every 250 feet (75 m) rise in altitude. Hill farmers know, often to their cost, of the variability from year to year of this important aspect. Data from the same station help to quantify the position. Between 1914 and 1956, the earliest date of "spring" growth was 3rd March and the latest was 3rd May, with a mean date of 13th April. Much of the more elevated Highlands experience a more rigorous climate than the Southern Uplands and, consequently, the lambing season (21st April to 31st May) can be well advanced before "spring" growth starts on many hills. The unreliability of weather at higher altitudes is often tragically underlined by the loss of life on the Scottish mountains in winter. Here, the weather can change from clear sunny skies to near-polar conditions in a matter of hours.

Topography

Although shelter and aspect are obviously important at the individual farm level, the dominant feature of topography nationally is the scarcity of arable (in-bye) land for growing winter feed, particularly for cattle. On hill farms, the proportion of arable ground is extremely limited (2%) being confined to fields along the valley floor and on the lower slopes where cultivation is possible. The risk of flooding in some areas means that soil capable of growing good crops is left for grazing only. In parts of the Highlands, potential arable land sometimes lies at the bottom of the lochs! The upland areas are less badly placed, with crops and grass averaging 22% of farm size, and the proportion is much more variable between districts and regions than for hill farming.

Soil

Although it is convenient to describe each physical factor separately, they are of course interdependent; this is particularly true of the formation and characteristics of soils, which are a function of both climate and relief. Relative to low-ground soils, hill soils are cold, wet and shallow. In addition to these physical limitations, many hills are deficient in the major plant nutrients (nitrogen, phosphorus and potassium) and most are highly acidic. Often in the hill situation it is not so much a question of lack of nutrients as of their being held in organic form, and thus unavailable for plant growth; this "locking up" is particularly so with nitrogen and phosphorus. The greatest stumbling block to widespread land improvement in the Scottish hills is acidity. Lime is a necessary precursor for all forms of land improvement involving fertilizers. In order to raise the pH-level, large quantities are required, and logistic difficulties arise where two or three tons of lime have to be applied per acre on hills difficult of access. Were it not so, large areas of hill grazings could be improved by aerial application of a few hundredweights of phosphate, as in New Zealand.

Under Scottish conditions, there is as yet no evidence of any limitation in the establishment or growth of improved pasture caused by trace-element deficiencies of a type known to occur elsewhere in the world, as for example in Australia. On the other hand, some hill soils, including peats, are known to be deficient in trace elements which, while not affecting pasture growth, give rise to deficiency conditions in the grazing animal.

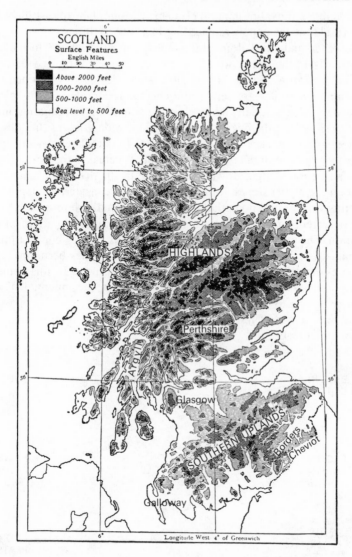

The improvement of hill swards and particularly liming (which will tend to decrease the availability of most trace elements) could, in some circumstances, aggravate or induce such conditions as *swayback* (copper deficiency) in lambs or *pine* (cobalt deficiency) in the grazing ruminant.

The inherent acidity arising from the high proportion of quartz in the parent material is reinforced by leaching of the more soluble base salts and by the biotic factor of animal grazing over centuries. The annual unavoidable removal of mineral elements through lambs, cast ewes and wool is seldom adequately replaced by lime and fertilizers.

The other, and allied, dominant factor is natural drainage. In the hills, particularly in the wetter west, the rate of disintegration and decay of organic substances (*humus*) is very slow where drainage is impeded. The raw humus (*mor*) is extremely acidic and unfavourable to most plants, other than those especially adapted to the conditions. Depending on the angle of slope and the degree of impediment, wide areas of the hills are covered with blanket peat of varying depth. In completely water-logged conditions *raised* or *basin* peat bogs develop. Whereas in the west, blanket peat can be found right down to sea-level, in the drier east it tends to occur on the higher slopes. Raised bogs, often of considerable depth, and sometimes over-lying potentially good arable land, are more limited in their occurrence and do not have a regular geographical pattern of distribution. The utilization and reclamation of this type of bog is a highly mechanised and specialized activity, and one which has been developed to a considerable extent in Eire and on the Continent. In this country, leaving aside some horticultural peat production, the potential of this resource has yet to be tapped.

The main types of hill soil in the context of land improvement are shown in figure 4·1.

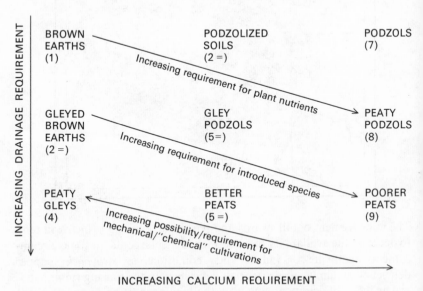

Figure 4.1 Land improvement techniques in relation to hill soils. Numbers in parentheses indicate ranking order for improvement, assuming choice available in a given situation (adapted from K. Simpson, 1974, unpublished).

Vegetation

In turn, the vegetational cover of the hills and uplands is dependent on soil, climate and altitude. Botanically, the Scottish hills have few species of plants relative to other ecosystems. This lack of floristic diversity means less flexibility, and the risk of overgrazing of the more acceptable species. The distribution of the various types of hill plants is determined largely by soil acidity and the degree of natural drainage. The relationships for six of the most common hill species are shown diagrammatically in figure 4.2.

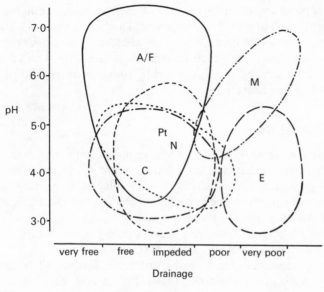

(1)	A/F	————	Agrostis/Fescue	(4)	E	—————	Eriophorum
(2)	C	—·—·—	Calluna	(5)	N	··········	Nardus
(3)	M	—··—··—	Molinia	(6)	Pt	————————	Pteridium

Figure 4.2 Ecological distribution of hill herbage, as defined by drainage and pH (adapted from D. J. Martin, 1974, unpublished).

It must be stressed that the shape and size of each area represents the range of tolerance to the two factors and *not* their relative proportions on the Scottish hills. Would that it were so! In cases where types overlap, the dominant plant is determined by other factors which include altitude, exposure and manipulation by man through grazing and burning.

Dividing the diagram horizontally at pH 4·5 gives in the upper half the less acid pastures with *Agrostis/Fescue* or *Molinia* dominant and in the lower half the acidic pastures with *Calluna, Nardus, Eriophorum* and *Pteridium*. Equally, a vertical axis through the impeded drainage point divides the pastures into drier areas of *Calluna, Agrostis/Fescue, Nardus* and *Pteridium* and the wetter pastures dominated by *Molinia* or *Eriophorum*.

In terms of usefulness to sheep the "ranking order" is as given in the legend. Their relative importance in the two predominant areas of hill and upland farming in Scotland—the Highlands and the Southern Uplands—is discussed in the following section dealing with techniques of land improvement. The British term *rough grazings*, which covers all the complex of plant communities on the hill, means an area of natural or semi-natural vegetation used by domesticated and other animals—mainly red deer and grouse—in contrast to areas where grass is considered as a crop. It is equivalent to the American term *range*. In Scotland no less than 73% of the total farming area is covered by rough grazings (11·2 million acres or 4·5 million hectares).

Improvement techniques

There is a wide range of techniques of land improvement to match the very varied conditions encountered. As shown in figure 4.3, they fall into two broad categories: (a) those which improve the value of the existing sward, and (b) those which involve the introduction of improved species. Broadly, the former are only used on those areas where the existing vegetation is of a relatively high quality, whereas areas of poor grazing require a more complex and more costly combination of treatments.

In farming terms, hill land suitable for improvement falls into two distinct types: *black* land and *green* land. For success, each calls for a distinctive approach which takes into account the physical nature of the terrain. Nor must the long-term economic aspects be overlooked. In the early days there was a tendency for this crucial issue to be submerged in a sea of technical enthusiasm.

The Highlands

Black land, so characteristic of much of the Highland landscape and at the lower end of the fertility spectrum, is typical acid moorland with varying depths of peat and normal associated flora: *Calluna, Erica, Molinia, Trichophorum, Eriophorum*, and *Sphagnum*. In areas of high rainfall and with slow movement of soil moisture, regeneration should always be concentrated on slopes. If flat areas or hollows are improved, the impeded

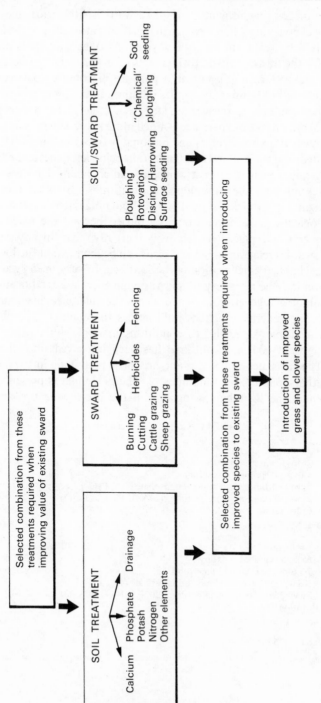

Figure 4.3 Summary of hill land improvement techniques (J. Frame, 1974, unpublished).

drainage means that in winter the new sward is little used due to the certainty of poaching.* If grazed, particularly by cattle, the poached sward is colonized by rushes in a very few years. Also, such a site is an ideal habitat for the freshwater snail which acts as a vector in the life cycle of the liver fluke (*Fasciola hepatica*), a parasite of considerable economic significance in hill farming. Examples of failure in the pioneering days to match the technique to the site are still to be seen in the higher-rainfall areas of Scotland. With experience, a much more successful mosaic pattern has emerged with knolls, ridges and reasonably free-draining slopes being regenerated, and the hollows and flat terrain being left undeveloped, other than by drainage where this is technically and economically feasible.

In black hill-land, the minimum of cultivation is advocated in order to avoid fragmenting the thin skin of "soil". Ploughing is detrimental, in that this biologically active layer would be buried beyond the reach of the seedlings and be replaced by relatively inert raw peat. In any case the original sward is relatively open and seeds can become established without undue mechanical amelioration of the seed bed. In very open swards, no cultivation may be necessary at all. Although there are modifications to the technique of regeneration to take account of differences in climate and soil type, the general principles hold across the country. The example detailed in Table 4.1 relates to conditions in Argyllshire, where some 49,000 acres (20,000 ha) of hill land has been improved since the early sixties. The costs, net of a 50% grant, are those pertaining in 1974.

In heather-dominant communities or where *Molinia* is present, over-burning and one light harrowing are all the pre-sowing preparations

Table 4.1   Cost of land reclamation

(i) *per acre*	
26 lb (12 kg) seeds mixture	£5·00
3 tons (3 t) ground limestone	13·00†
6 cwt (300 kg) ground mineral phosphate (40% P_2O_5)	7·50†
2 cwt (100 kg) compound fertilizer (20N:10P_2O_5:10K_2O)	2·50†
Cultivations	2·00
Total Net Cost	£30·00
(ii) *per hectare*	
65 lb (30 kg) seeds mixture	£12·50
7·5 tons (7·5 t) ground limestone	32·50
15 cwt (750 kg) ground mineral phosphate (40% P_2O_5)	18·75
5 cwt (250 kg) compound fertilizer (20N:10P_2O_5:10K_2O)	6·25
Cultivations	5·00
Total Net Cost	£75·00

† Including spreading costs.

* Poaching: severe damage to the sward due to stock trampling under very wet or water-logged conditions.

required. After sowing, one pass with a roller gives sufficient consolidation. The seeds mixture comprises 2 lb of white clover (*Trifolium repens*, var. *Grasslands Huia* or *Aberystwyth S100*) and equal proportions of perennial ryegrass (*Lolium perenne*), cocksfoot (*Dactylis glomerata*) and timothy (*Phleum pratense*). The varieties of clover have been found to be more productive than wild white under Argyllshire conditions. The grass seeds mixture contains early and late-growing strains in order to extend the growing season by two weeks at either end. Given good management and proper maintenance, the pasture should last for many years, but with a gradual loss of vigour in the sown species. Nor is the improvement confined to the treated acres. The mosaic pattern encourages animals to range and to improve the untreated areas through their grazing and excreta. The importance of "the golden hoof" for maintaining fertility in the lowlands has been recognized for centuries. Studies by the Hill Farming Research Organisation (H.F.R.O.) have shown that nutrient re-cycling via the grazing animal is no less important on the hill.

On the green land where grasses predominate, the technique varies, depending on the degree of acidity. In *Agrostis/Festuca* areas where indigenous white clover is present, dressings of lime and phosphate may be sufficient. On more-acid soils, beyond the tolerance of clover, rotovation and reseeding are necessary. Due to the closer and tougher sward, pre-sowing cultivations need to be more rigorous than on black land. The seeds mixture and fertilizer treatment are broadly as before but, due to the extra cultivation required, the net cost in 1974 would be around £35 per acre (£88/ha). Also, due to much better natural drainage on the mineral soil, and consequently a faster rate of leaching, maintenance dressings need to be more frequent. In some instances a moderate dressing of a compound fertilizer may be given annually. Although more expensive to establish and maintain, it does not follow that these grassy reseeded areas are less economic over their productive life. On the contrary, they are higher up the fertility scale of hill vegetation and, other things remaining equal, will be a more productive subject in the long term than the black land.

The Southern Uplands

In the Southern Uplands, the proportion of green hills is very much greater than in the Highlands. As we move from west to east, the rainfall and the coverage of blanket peat decline. The severely glaciated hills and moorlands of Galloway give way to the drier rolling hills of the Border country. The region is naturally more productive than the rugged mountains of the north and west of the country. Relatively speaking, the need for land improvement is less obvious, and the economic spur less sharp. Nevertheless, hills which have been subjected to selective grazing by sheep for almost 600 years, compared to two centuries in the Highlands, must offer considerable scope for up-grading. This has been amply demonstrated by the H.F.R.O. on the Cheviot Hills. On many farms, considerable areas of hill land have been improved without the need for the introduction of improved grass and clover species. Regeneration of the existing sward is significantly cheaper than reclamation with its extra cultivation and seed costs. Burning, draining and applying lime and/or slag are the oldest and commonest practices in the Southern Uplands. The long-term response to these techniques depends largely on the status of the soil, the composition of the herbage, and management of the livestock. The control of bracken, a serious problem on some of the best soils of these hills, is detailed in a later section. In the season following a profitable year, the amount spent on liming and/or slagging is significant. With the introduction of new methods of steel production, the supply of basic slag, a source of phosphate, is dwindling. Low-grade slag, with its considerable content of calcium, was very useful to the hill farmer. Today it has had to be largely replaced by ground mineral phosphate, and separate lime applications are necessary.

Research, both in Wales and Scotland, has shown that once a move is made off the best subjects onto the poorer types of grassy pasture—*Nardus* or *Molinia*-dominated swards—improvement by lime or fertilizer application is often too slow to be of practical and economic benefit, and re-seeding is necessary. In contrast to the Highlands, the deeper and freer-draining mineral soil and the gentler contour permit of greater use of the plough. Until the recent introduction of the rotovator, the plough was the main implement of improvement. Ploughing, by virtual elimination of competition from the existing sward species, is the quickest way of preparing the ground for the introduction and early establishment of the improved seeds mixture. It also leaves a uniform land surface, which is important if the improved area is intended as an in-bye field from which hay or silage may be taken in the future.

Rotovation, which is less expensive than ploughing, is another technique which allows a quick establishment in areas of dense existing swards. It is also more flexible in that the degree of suppression required can be controlled. With the fluffy seed bed produced by the rotovator, particular care has to be taken in choice of time of sowing to avoid the risk, present in all forms of reseeding, of "drying out" of the young seedlings—due to a temporary but critical shortage of soil moisture. Various forms of harrow, but increasingly the disc type, represent the minimum form of cultivation on close grassy swards. They reduce but do not eliminate competition.

In the last two decades, chemical alternatives to mechanical cultivation have been available. Herbicides, such as dalapon and paraquat, can give partial or complete destruction of the sward. Although used to good effect in specific situations, e.g. on *Nardus* or *Molinia*-dominant areas in the East Border hills, "chemical ploughing" has not proved generally satisfactory in the hill country; perhaps not surprisingly since grass-killing herbicides are most effective on short green actively-growing swards! Also, in the cold often-highly-organic soils, there can be a danger of residual toxicity leading to poor seed establishment. Another recent innovation is sod-seeding. Basically, this method of partial cultivation consists of gouging-out narrow slits at intervals across a grassy sward with a sod-seeder. The machine deposits the seed and fertilizer in the same operation. Under British conditions, the technique has not as yet lived up to the promise shown abroad. The tighter-knit swards encountered here give much stronger competition to the sown species. Both techniques have no relevance on black hill land.

With the continuous decline in the labour force, the general need for fencing has become more pressing. For land improvement specifically, the full benefit can only be reaped through judicious control of grazing on the improved area. Automatically, this means some measure of control "on the other side of the fence", viz. the open hill. Without fencing, a small acreage of reseeded land can be quickly reduced by over-stocking to a condition worse than that prior to treatment. In the mosaic pattern there is no question of fencing off the individual reseeded areas, but it is desirable that the area of the hill in which they are situated is enclosed. The proportion of the directly treated area to the total enclosure varies, depending on the site; under Argyllshire conditions, around 25% is not uncommon. Provided that a sufficiently large acreage is done, the need for fencing is not so important in cases where only lime and fertilizer are involved.

In the Southern Uplands, a "rule of thumb" guide is: not less than 50 acres in aggregate, and laid down in such a way that sheep will be encouraged to graze the area uniformly. The Southern Uplands, historically and still today, have a further advantage in terms of enclosures. There, the majority of hill and upland farms are ring-fenced, often in the form of stone dykes, whereas in the Highlands open marches are the rule. Clearly, the possession of a boundary fence is of cardinal importance in any scheme of land improvement which has as its ultimate aim a significant upward shift in the overall grazing potential, leading to a bigger and/or better sheep stock.

Unfortunately, the cost of fencing has risen very steeply in the past two years. Current quotations for the traditional hill fence are of the order of 75–80p gross per yard. A net cost of £700 per mile (£435/km) can be a stumbling block! Where the terrain allows, the cheaper form of high-tensile fence lowers the cost to 40–50p gross per yard. Over the years since the 1946 Hill Farming Act, Government assistance towards the cost of various forms of improvement has been of paramount importance. There have been several different schemes with varying rates of grant. Currently, all forms of land improvement in the hills and uplands attract a 50% subsidy other than drainage (70% of approved cost). Fencing, the key to any real improvement in the hills, should merit at least as high a rate, even if this extra support were at the expense of other forms of subsidy which do not contribute *per se* to increased production in the future. Even a slight shift in emphasis, from support via headage subsidies (e.g. on hill ewes and hill cows) to increased aid through improvement grants, would seem more promising in the long term.

Structure of the hill and upland sector

It is clear that the structure, organization and management of hill and upland farms are to a large degree determined—particularly in the case of the former—by the poverty of the organic resources and by the adverse climate relative to lowland farming. These factors govern the types of livestock and crop, and the extent to which stocking and cropping is possible. Within these limits, economic factors determine the organization and method of management.

Table 4.2(i) demonstrates the importance of the hill and upland sector in terms of land use. Although it has only a quarter of the full-time farms in Scotland, it covers nine-tenths of the rough grazings and contains almost three-quarters of the national sheep flock and over half of the Scottish beef herd. The hill farms are the main reservoir of sheep, whereas the upland farms are much more important as a source of beef cattle supplies.

Part (ii) illustrates the consequences of the dominant physical factors. It should be stressed, however, that these are national averages and that there are wide variations (particularly in the stock-carrying capacity of the hills) between regions, and differences between districts. As a broad guide at regional level, the stock-carrying capacity of the majority of the hills in the Southern Uplands is 2 to 3 acres per ewe; the Central Highlands 3 to 4 acres, and the North-West Highlands 8 to 12 acres. Nevertheless, the figures do show the principal features: the very small proportion (2%) of low ground, and the wide ratio of ewes to cows on the hill farm; the better proportion of low ground (22%) and the increasing importance of cattle on the upland farm. As the difference, especially in the context of land improvement, between the two types of farming is largely one of degree, the remainder of this section relates to hill farming.

Table 4.2

(i) Basic Structure of Hill and Upland Farms in Scotland, as at June 1973. (Adapted from Agricultural Statistics 1973 Scotland, H.M.S.O.) Percentages relate to full-time Scottish totals.

Farm type	No. of farms	%	Rough grazings '000 acres	%	Breeding ewes '000	%	Beef cows '000	%
Hill	1307	6·3	5417	61	1128	41·0	42	9·3
Upland	4158	20·2	2600	29	893	32·4	202	44·9
Combined	5465	26·5	8017	90	2021	73·4	244	54·2

(ii) Average Size and Stocking Rates of Farms at National Level. (Adapted from Agricultural Statistics 1973 Scotland, H.M.S.O.)

	Hill farm		Upland farm	
Crops and grass	96*	(39)	181	(73)
Rough grazings	4144	(1677)	625	(253)
Total area	4240	(1716)	806	(326)
No. of ewes	863		215	
No. of cows	32		49	
Rough grazing per ewe	4·8	(1·9)	2·9	(1·2)
No. of ewes per cow	27·0		4·4	

* Acres (ha in parentheses).

Notes 1. Figures relate to full-time farming units only; crofts and other part-time units are excluded, as are common grazings.

2. The table is based on the Department of Agriculture and Fisheries for Scotland (D.A.F.S.) classification.

Economic implications

In hill sheep production, where the majority of lambs are sold as *stores* (i.e. requiring further finishing on lowland farms) the volume of and return from output per acre is very low, and consequently the size of the production unit (i.e. the farm) must be large if a worth-while return is to be obtained. This tends to force sheep rearing out on to the extensive areas of high-lying less-productive, and hence cheaper, land. On the hill farm, the scope for manoeuvre in response to economic change is extremely limited, for the scarcity of arable ground to grow fodder restricts to a large extent the number of beef cattle which can be carried, whether indoors or out, unless resort is made to outside sources of hay. The imbalance between fodder supplies and cattle numbers—leading to abnormally high levels of hay prices (£60–£80 per ton)—in the more remote areas of the hills and uplands of Britain in the winter of 1974/75 illustrates dramatically the danger of becoming over-dependent on purchased supplies. Although hill cows made a valuable contribution to farm profitability, particularly on the smaller hill farm, they can only be regarded as a supplementary line of production.

Environment has imposed specialization on the hill-farming industry, and certain economic disadvantages stem from this. There can be no spreading of risks over several products, and there is marked seasonality of production. Excluding the receipt of various subsidy payments, almost all the annual revenue is received in late August, September and October through the sale of store lambs, cast ewes, wool, and weaned calves. In contrast to the dairy farmer, with his monthly milk cheque, the hill farmer does not enjoy the advantages of a regular inflow of working capital. This irregular cash-flow pattern is of significance when contemplating the funding of any major form of land improvement.

Again, due to the lack of in-bye land and climate, all sheep (other than the breeding flock and their replacements) must be sold before the onset of winter. Consequently, there can be no regulating of supply when demand is weak, and this can give rise to wide fluctuations in prices at auction markets. The level of demand for store animals is dependent on the many national and international considerations affecting lowland farming, where the final fattening takes place. The complex question of the highly stratified Scottish sheep industry is outwith the scope of an essay on land improvement, although it has a vital bearing on the profitability of the breeding sector. It must be stressed, however, that hill and upland producers, with their heavy dependence on store animals, are more vulnerable to the cyclical fluctuations in the national sheep and cattle populations; and these movements have a strong influence on store prices over time.

Another key characteristic of hill farming is its vulnerability to wide annual fluctuations in volume of output, largely as a concomitant of weather, particularly in winter and spring. Seasonal effects are most clearly seen in the annual level of the lamb crop, as conventionally measured in terms of the *lamb marking percentage*, i.e. the number of lambs surviving at June expressed as a percentage of ewes mated the previous December. Veterinary investigations have shown that, under West Highland conditions, around 90% of the ewes are pregnant in March, but by June the effective lamb crop is down by 15%–20%, due largely to deaths at birth or shortly thereafter. Lambing in an improved enclosure can mitigate the effect of this annual drain on productivity. Figure 4.4 shows the long-period trend from a largely identical sample of about 30 hill farms in the Highland region of the West of Scotland College province.

The equivalent figures from a similar but smaller sample of about 20 hill farms in the Southern Uplands over the same time ranged from 81% in 1969 to 105% in 1959 with an annual mean of 92%. The death rate in ewes

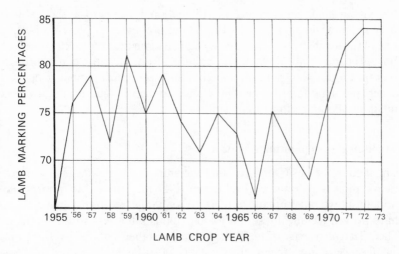

Figure 4.4 Average lamb crop levels on West Highland hill farms, 1955–73 inclusive (West of Scotland Agricultural College, Economics Division).

and the weight of the wool clip are also affected but, apart from seasons of exceptional snow-fall, the results are not so drastic. Investigations have shown that land improvement may modify but does not insulate a sheep flock from these seasonal effects.

Although no one would deny that environmental factors, and especially climate, are much more limiting in the hills than in the lowlands of Scotland, they do not represent a particularly unusual set of circumstances in world terms. Ranching in the High Plains of the United States, the sheep stations in the drought-risk areas of Australia, and the high country in New Zealand are but three examples in this category.

The size of farm is also important, and increasingly so as the years pass. The structure of hill and upland farming in Scotland is stronger than in most other hill areas of the United Kingdom. Nevertheless, farms which historically were of adequate size to give a reasonable standard of living are now coming under increasing pressure, through ever-rising costs, in providing a profit sufficient for living expenses let alone savings for capital investment in improvements (see Table 4.3).

With the current record level of interest rates (14–16% on bank over-drafts), the ability to fund capital for expansion from within the business is more important than it was in the past. Over the twelve-year period from 1956–1967 the annual rate of bank overdraft interest averaged $7\frac{1}{2}\%$.

In the absence of any significant structural reform as yet through national incentive schemes, an increase in turnover of the farm business is the only avenue. The expansion in the national beef herd in the last two decades, in which all sectors of the agricultural industry played a part, is one of the most striking changes in Scottish agriculture since the war. For hill sheep, any radical change in volume of output must come through modification of the traditional method of sheep grazing management. It is here that land improvement in relation to the whole farm situation has much to offer in certain circumstances.

Traditional system of management

The land is the basic resource, and the animals are the means by which man exploits the resource. Until recently, the majority of hill farmers had no alternative but to manage their flocks along traditional lines, which have proved technically sound for the animals but less so for the land. The selective over-grazing of the more palatable herbage by sheep. in the absence of a complementary balance of cattle, has led over the centuries to a gradual deterioration in the type and value of the vegetational cover.

The traditional and still by far the most common method of hill flock management in Scotland is based on the *hefting* instinct. This strong sense of territory, highly developed in hill breeds of sheep, makes possible a system of farming on the extensive, often remote and unfenced areas of rough grazings. The *heft* is a natural geographic sub-division of the hill, and several hefts constitute a *hirsel*, which historically was the area and the number of ewes under the care of one shepherd. The continuing drift of labour from the land has not by-passed the hills. The scarcity of shepherds, particularly young skilled men, is a serious problem and one which is bringing the traditional system—of set stocking on the hill all the year round—under increasing stress. The acreage of ground to be covered by one man varies widely between regions, as it has always done due to physical and managerial factors, but in all regions it is much higher today than in former times.

If the system is not to break down, the shepherd and his dog must be reinforced by fencing, at least at certain peak times of labour demand. The extreme alternative (*ranching*) of one man looking after upwards of 1000 ewes cannot be defended on either long-term economic or social grounds, although it has alluring short-term but short-lived cost-saving prospects! Land improvement of the type described earlier has an important part to play in easing the labour problem. At mating time (21st November to 31st December), and again at lambing (21st April to 31st May), an improved enclosure to hold the ewe flock has obvious advantages, with considerably less physical effort on the part of the shepherd. Even at a stocking rate of around three acres per ewe, a hirsel of 600 ewes means some 1800 acres (730 ha) and implies a considerable expenditure of time and energy in getting around the hill. These "service areas" are now becoming more common, although mating and lambing on the open hill is still the general rule. The major role, however, of improved and enclosed areas lies in the better control, utilization and productivity of the whole hill resource. In short, where it is technically sound and economically feasible, the enclosure should be a means to an end and not an end in itself.

In the traditional system it is not customary to hand-feed hill flocks, except in periods of severe weather. The ewes are wholly dependent on rough grazings throughout the year, and thus the level of stocking is determined by the capacity of the hill to support the ewes in winter at a tolerable level of nutrition. Inevitably, this leads to a considerable under-utilization of pasture growth in summer, and to an accumulation of ungrazed material which quickly declines in feeding value. This imbalance between the grazing pressure of sheep and the highly seasonal nature of pasture growth on the hill has important but unfavourable consequences on the annual cycle of nutrition.

Research

Since the foundation of the Hill Farming Research Organization (H.F.R.O.) in 1953, research into the fundamental aspects of the grazing behaviour of sheep on open range, of the response of hill vegetation to different grazing regimes, and of the inter-related components of animal nutrition has shed considerable light on the problem. Such a biological analysis of hill sheep production is a necessary prerequisite if sound alternatives to the traditional system are to be developed and taken up by the industry on any significant scale. This considerable input of research effort not only quantified in scientific terms some familiar problems, but also revealed new aspects of hill sheep production which formerly were not widely recognized as limiting in the all-pervading light of the "winter-gap" in nutrition. In brief, the potential of hill grazing is low—about one-fifth of that of lowland grass—but the poor utilization pattern means that only 20–30% of the grass actually grown is ingested by sheep. This in turn leads to a poor cyclical pattern of animal nutrition (which is limiting not only in winter but in varying degrees throughout the whole breeding cycle) due to poor-quality herbage. Each seasonal link in the nutritional chain influences the one following, and summer and autumn are as important nutritionally as the well-known winter and spring periods. The hardy breeds of hill sheep depend on their body reserves to come through the winter in-lamb on a very low plane of nutrition. Any improvement in summer nutrition, leading to better body condition at mating (and hence higher conception rates) and throughout the early winter, is of special significance in widening the winter bottle-neck.

Development of new systems

As a consequence of this work, H.F.R.O. on their own stations, the three Scottish Colleges of Agriculture on their hill farms, and a number of pioneering hill farmers have been developing new systems of husbandry under a wide range of conditions. Considerable development work is also going forward at the Ministry of Agriculture's experimental husbandry farms in the North of England and Wales. In all cases some measure of land improvement, grazing control, and increased stocking are the basic ingredients. This development has come to be known as the *two-sward system*. There is nothing new in the principle of establishing small high-quality areas in a range of overall low value. An obvious example is the small but very valuable area of in-bye land on most hill farms. What is novel about the system is that the improved enclosure is out on the hill, and is designed to be utilized by the whole breeding flock at key times of the year. The overall aim is to match more closely the pattern of pasture growth to the nutritional needs of the sheep.

Technically, the basic essentials of this two-sward technique are the correct selection and size of the enclosure in relation to the hill, the choice and proportion of the areas to be improved within the enclosure, and the optimum grazing pressure in the enclosure at those parts of the season which will give the maximum boost to production without undermining the enclosure, the hill or, in the longer term, the health and productivity of the stock. Although there are minor regional modifications, generally the ewe flock grazes the enclosure(s) prior to and over the mating period, and then returns to the unimproved hill from New Year until the approach of lambing. It is essential in this system to give supplementary feed in late pregnancy. The ewes and their lambs remain in the enclosure, in order to take full advantage of the improved pasture during the important lactation phase. Barren ewes and ewe hoggs are summered on the hill. After weaning in mid-August, the area is rested in order to allow recovery of the sward in time for the start of the next breeding cycle. Under the two-sward system, a high proportion of twin lambs is a valuable asset rather than the embarrassment it is in the traditional system.

Although sheep are the dominant enterprise on Scottish hill farms, cattle can play a very valuable part in the control of grazing, both in and outwith the enclosure. There were strong economic forces acting in favour of cattle, relative to sheep, for a long period until the beef crisis in 1974, and in many instances provision must be made for the rotational grazing of both classes of livestock in the system.

There is a wealth of scientific data in the published literature, but as yet a dearth of economic results, in depth and in farm management terms, about actual case studies. This is mainly due to the early stage of development of the technique, but through the Scottish Agricultural Development Council steps have now been taken by the Scottish Colleges in consultation with H.F.R.O. to monitor over the next five years at least, the technical and economic progress of development projects initiated on a small sample of commercial farms in the winter of 1974/75. This combined approach should help to swell the pool of knowledge.

The financial background

Technical achievement and financial success do not always go hand-in-hand. The former can be easily demonstrated in most forms of land improvement; the latter is more difficult to disentangle from the web of complex factors affecting the hill-farming industry. The degree of difficulty varies with the type of improvement and the two-sward technique by its very nature is a longer-term process than most. This means that it is more vulnerable to sudden changes in the relationship between costs and product prices during the years before it is fully established than are the more conventional forms of reclamation on a hill farm. The trend in profitability shown in Table 4.3 illustrates this point. Should the relationship deteriorate dramatically as in 1974, the "pay-back" period is prolonged.

Table 4.3 *Profitability of Scottish Hill Farms: National Averages of Net Income Per Farm, 1950–75.* (Figures from Scottish Agricultural Economics, Vols I–XXV, H.M.S.O.)

	£		£		£
1950	710	1960	812	1970	1736
1951	819	1961	1097	1971	3831
1952	938	1962	832	1972	5360
1953	1059	1963	1593	1973	6137
1954	784	1964	1676	1974	3000*
1955	912	1965	1372	1975	4500†
1956	1154	1966	776		
1957	1596	1967	1322		
1958	1253	1968	1470		
1959	1144	1969	1163		
Decade Average	1037		1211		

* Author's estimate. † Author's forecast.

As part of the United Kingdom Price Review requirements, the three Scottish Colleges of Agriculture are responsible for the annual collection of financial data from representative samples of the main types of farming in Scotland. The figures in Table 4.3 are national averages from the hill sheep farm sample. The majority of the farms have been in the sample over the 26-year period, although the number has varied around a mean of 82 per annum. In 1973/74, the last year for which published figures are available, the average stocking was 942 ewes and 27 cows on 3400 acres (1380 ha), only 90 (36 ha) of which were crops and grass.

For present purposes Net Income can be taken as being equivalent to Net Profit. Owner-occupied farms are converted to a tenancy basis; no charge has been made at this stage for the farmer's manual work, nor for interest on capital, and finally the basis of livestock valuation over the years has always been conservative market value.

Remembering that Net Profit has to cover personal drawings and Income Tax, it is clear that the scope for accumulation of capital on the *average* hill farm was limited until the early seventies. Also, because of the marked increase in sheep and cattle prices from 1971 through to 1973, the values of breeding livestock were also increasing, and consequently a significant proportion of the Net Profit was in a non-cash form or "paper profit". (In 1973, £1370.)

The figures as they stand do not tell the whole story, for the purchasing power of the £ was falling throughout the period, and at an increasing rate in the seventies. Using the Retail Price Index, with 1952 as the base year, a series of indices were prepared and applied to the actual Net Profit figures. This gave the annual profit levels in terms of the purchasing power of the £ as at 1952. This conversion to *real terms* was illuminating.

In the decade of the fifties, the overall picture was one of relative stability in real terms, with the latter half showing improvement in both actual and real terms. Lamb crop year 1957 was long remembered by flockmasters, and rightly so, for it was not until 1971 that there was a better year in terms of purchasing power. The decade of the sixties was much poorer than that of the fifties, and very unstable. From 1970 on there was a strong upward movement, culminating in 1973 in the best hill-farming year since the war. It must be stressed that the 1974 figure is very much an estimate, but even if it is understated, it is clear that in real terms the 1974 season will have been one of the worst.

The future?

It is far too early to be sanguine about the eventual outcome of this new technique of hill-land management. Certainly, the technical results to date from all the centres, both in terms of increased productivity per ewe and increased stock-carrying capacity, are very encouraging. On the financial side also, the position is not without promise—particularly in those projects which were started several years ago, when the amount and cost of capital required was considerably lower; the tide of profitability was flowing strongly during the establishment years until 1974. The position is much less favourable for those starting now. Establishment and extra running costs have escalated compared to five years ago and, if 1974 product prices are any guide, the cost/price relationship in future could mean considerable cash flow difficulties in the early years of a project. In such a situation "make haste slowly" must be the motto. Prior to 1974, the scene seemed set at last for a period of profits on a higher plateau than formerly, but that season's results have considerably shaken confidence in any form of improvement, whether on the hill or elsewhere. Despite this set-back one remains optimistic in the medium and long term. Down the vale of the years there have been many examples, in industry as well as in agriculture, where a technical breakthrough was not widely endorsed for several years after its introduction, often on grounds of cost.

In closing, it must be stressed that the two-sward system is still at the development stage. The number of farmers practising this system is as yet insignificant, and much has still to be learned about its application across the wide spectrum of climatic and soil conditions on the Scottish hills. Looking to the future it is clear that hill farmers will need to become as skilful in the management of hill pastures as they are in the handling of their flocks. The need to control the grazing is fundamental, and this is easier to do within the enclosure than on the remaining 75–85% of unimproved hill. On poor soils in high-rainfall areas there can be a vegetational trend—under the traditional system—away from heather towards *Molinia* and *Trichophorum*. A more intensive grazing system may aggravate this trend on the hill. To exchange heather, a very useful source of winter feed, for *Molinia* and *Trichophorum*, both of which are useless to sheep in winter, would be a costly mistake. The impression remains that the new system is more promising on the drier and better soils of the Southern Uplands, parts of the East Highlands, and parts of south Argyll. The West and North-West Highlands would not seem to be well placed for the establishment of a high-input/high-output system which would remain stable over time. From an economic viewpoint, the danger must be avoided of a treadmill pattern developing in which costly renewals are needed in an attempt to attain stability in a situation where, due to the climate and the poverty of the organic resources, such attainment may be impossible.

If a new technique of hill-grazing management, whether it be the two-sward system or some other form of rotational grazing, is technically sound both in agricultural and ecological terms, then it offers at least an alternative to the traditional system, which does not allow the hill breeds of sheep to realize their full potential. When, where and to what extent this approach will be followed, will be largely determined by economic factors far removed from the hillside.

BRACKEN CONTROL

With the possible exception of heather, the bracken fern is the one plant on the hillside most easily recognized by city dwellers. The banners of green in summer, when the fronds are fully extended, and the freckles of brown in autumn, when the fronds have turned to litter, are familiar to many and aesthetically pleasing to a few. For those who earn their living from the hills, the view is different.

Historical background

Bracken (*Pteridium aquilinum*) is one of the most widely distributed plants in the world and is of very ancient lineage; evidence from fossil spores would indicate some two million years. Before man had the ability to alter his vegetational environment, bracken was a plant of deciduous woodlands where the tree canopy was not dense. Some 5000 years ago, Neolithic man by his "fire clearings" began the process of denudation of the tree cover. The bracken plant with its extensive system of *underground* stems (rhizomes) was little damaged by fire, whereas its competitors on the forest floor were severely checked or destroyed. When the soil became impoverished by continuous cropping, man moved on to new areas. The fern, with its massive reserve of carbohydrates stored in the rhizomes, was well placed to become the dominant plant in the abandoned clearings.

Over the millenia, the exchange of trees for plants more useful to man has continued at an accelerating rate. However, as man's skill as a toolmaker developed and his knowledge of farming grew, the pattern slowly changed. The invention of the plough, and the discovery of the advantages of growing crops in rotation, marked the beginning of the end for bracken as a dominant plant on land suitable for cultivation. The plough, by breaking up and bringing the rhizome mat to the surface, is still the cheapest and best eradicant of bracken on arable land. Thus it is that today, bracken infestation is almost exclusively confined to the hills and uplands.

There is ample evidence that bracken was not always regarded as a weed. On the industrial side, because the fronds are rich in potassium, bracken ash was a source of alkali essential for glass making, linen bleaching and soap production, but the chemical synthesis of pure alkali in 1837 saw the end of this phase. Prior to 1914, Germany was a major supplier of potassium fertilizer, and the outbreak of the 1914–18 war gave a short-lived stimulus to the use of bracken as a fertilizer in Britain.

On the agricultural side, the utility of the fern was not so episodic and much more widespread. For example, in the Highlands of Scotland there is ample evidence that bracken was a valuable resource, particularly under the clan system of land settlement. In a close-knit community and within a largely subsistence economy, the need to exploit all possible indigenous resources was pressing. Bracken fronds provided bedding for both man and beast, thatch for the homestead and, on occasion, fuel for the fire. From the point of view of bracken control, harvesting of fronds for those purposes would be far too late in the season (autumn) to have any marked ecological effect. Logic would suggest that sustained yield rather than control was the objective. At this time, cattle were the main source of meat and of exchange, and the Highland glens carried a large population of cattle as well as people. There is a contention, oft repeated, that cattle, by virtue of their heavier weight and less selective grazing habits compared to sheep, played a large part in preventing the spread of bracken. In a fenced enclosure, stocked at a high density per acre and receiving supplementary feeding, it is true that cattle can reduce bracken infestation to negligible proportions. The unenclosed hills and glens of eighteenth-century Scotland are a somewhat different proposition!

The defeat of the predominantly Highland army at Culloden in 1745 started off a chain of events which was to alter the cultural, social and economic face of the Highlands. There was a traumatic change in land use when the clansmen were forced to leave the glens, either to emigrate or settle on much less favourable areas (the present-day crofting townships) on the coastal fringe. Depopulation and the replacement of a relatively intensive system (based on cattle) by an extensive system (based almost exclusively on sheep) meant that bracken was no longer needed in any significant quantity. In short, its status fell from a useful resource to a useless weed.

This change in land use is often cited as the main cause of the reputed spread of bracken in the Highlands over the past two centuries. The evidence on the effect of "cropping" the bracken and on control by cattle seems unconvincing. All would agree, however, that the abandoned strips of cultivated land in the glen would be quickly colonized by the fern. On the hill, the introduction of the Southern Upland flockmasters' practice of burning the grass in spring to get rid of the accumulated mat of dead vegetation and to stimulate grass growth would be another important factor in areas where bracken was present. In a mixed community of heather and bracken, the latter, possessing the same morphological advantage as its ancestor in the primeval forest, would oust the former. The degree to which each of the many inter-related factors contributed to the spread of the fern in the Highlands after the arrival of the sheep some two centuries ago, will never be known. That bracken is now a serious weed on the hills and uplands of Scotland is beyond question. It is one of the most important technical problems—as distinct from economic problems affecting hill farming as an industry—coming second only to the wider aspect of grazing control on the hill.

Ecological preferences and distribution

In 1957 the first and only attempt to quantify the extent of the problem for the whole of Scotland was carried out by the Department of Agriculture for Scotland through the medium of the June Agricultural Census. The total estimate was 450,000 acres (180,000 ha), no less than 98% of which was on rough grazings. Of more moment is the distribution. The census data clearly confirmed that the bracken problem is largely one of the South and West. Over 50% of the total acreage was contained in six of the 33 counties: Argyllshire in the West Highlands, plus the five counties stretching across the Southern Uplands from Wigtown to Selkirk. The effect of cultivation by man has virtually eliminated bracken from arable land, and hence the much lower degree of infestation on the eastern side of Scotland, the major cropping area. On the hills and uplands, the ecological preferences of the plant have largely determined its distribution. The fern, which is acid-tolerant, prefers a deep but free-draining soil. Given that drainage is not impeded, bracken can thrive in areas of very high rainfall. Although it grows on open hillsides, the fern prefers a sheltered site, as the fronds are vulnerable to high winds. Hence the strongest stands of bracken are to be found on the lower slopes of the glens. In contrast, the large expanse of wet plateau in the North-West Highlands is not conducive to widespread growth. The altitudinal zone for bracken in Scotland is from sea-level to around the 1600 ft contour (490 m).

Morphological advantages

In addition to the massive underground reserves of carbohydrate, the bracken plant has three further advantages in the struggle for dominance. Like all members of the fern family, reproduction can be either sexual or asexual, depending on the micro-climate. The former requires conditions not generally found on the hillside. Consequently, the spread of bracken is nearly always the result of vegetational reproduction via an extension of the rhizome system. Dormant buds on the rhizomes near the surface can develop into new fronds to replace any which have been damaged or destroyed. Thirdly, the fronds form a canopy over their smaller competitors and reduce the light intensity. The degree to which useful grasses are present under the canopy depends on the density and height of the fronds. In a heavy stand of bracken there may be virtually no other plants; only the accumulated litter from previous seasons on top of brown earth. This covering protects the next season's emerging frond shoots which are vulnerable to late spring frosts.

From an ecological point of view, it is clear that bracken is a well-adapted long-established and very powerful competitor, and from the standpoint of hill farming, a difficult problem to overcome. When the parameter of economics is introduced, the problem becomes formidable! Within the bounds of prudent capital investment, there is as yet no answer to the problem of complete eradication on the hills and uplands. All that can be done—and only in certain situations—is some measure of acceptable control of the bracken canopy to the extent that it is not inhibiting useful grazing of the sward by livestock. On the drier hills at the eastern end of the Southern Uplands, a light canopy of bracken can be beneficial in certain seasons. In the spring there is an "early bite" of grass, and in a hot summer the grass in the bracken areas is less liable to desiccation. In the milder and wetter west, however, little is to be heard in defence of bracken.

The significance of the problem

In 1957 there were some 450,000 acres (180,000 ha) affected by bracken, or approximately 4% of the total area of rough grazing in Scotland. The main change in land use in the intervening years in the hills and uplands has been the continuing swing to afforestation. Assuming that the degree of infestation on land acquired for forestry was of the same order as on the remainder, the acreage in 1974 would be of the order of 400,000 acres (160,000 ha). In view of the ecological preferences of the plant, it is clear that on many hills and glens bracken occupies some of the best soils. The problem, from the farmer's viewpoint, is therefore far more serious than is indicated by a simple quantitative approach. Many farmers, who have been active in bracken control over the years, are of the opinion that one acre of bracken-cleared land is worth several acres higher up the hill, particularly in the early spring. Even at a factor of $2\frac{1}{2}$, this is equivalent to an extra million acres of rough grazing. The hill and upland sector of the agricultural industry in Scotland could be said to be operating at some-where below 10% of potential capacity due to bracken alone. The actual proportion would depend on the degree of infestation; in dense stands of bracken the agricultural contribution is negligible.

Methods of control

In tackling this serious problem there are three methods of approach:

(a) dense stocking within enclosures
(b) cutting
(c) chemical control by a selective herbicide.

In commercial terms, significant reduction of the bracken canopy by dense stocking is out of the question under Scottish conditions. Until the recent introduction of acceptable herbicides, the only feasible methods were cutting, slashing or bruising the fronds. The principle behind all three is the same: namely, annual defoliation over several seasons to reduce and weaken the plant. The time of cutting is crucial. Under West of Scotland conditions, the most effective time is around the last week in June. By then the fronds are almost fully extended but have not yet started to pass back carbohydrate to the rhizome for storage. In brief, control is by systematic depletion of the plant's reserves over a time. Two cuts per season have been found to be more effective, and the second cut is generally given some six weeks after the first, to remove the replacement fronds arising from the later developing and dormant buds. For generations the scythe was the major weapon. During the 1939/45 war self-propelled machines were fairly common. Later improvement in tractor design provided another powerful tool in the struggle against bracken.

In the early fifties there was a rekindling of interest in bracken control. In 1952 two large-scale trials of four tractor-operated machines were set up, one in Roxburghshire and the other in Perthshire. The trials were a combined effort by agricultural engineers, botanists and economists, as well as the key men in such situations, the farmers.

A botanical and economic case study

At the Perthshire site where some 450 acres (180 ha) were treated, three years of double "cutting" plus a single treatment in 1955, gave an average reduction in frond height of 80% and an average reduction in density of 75%. At the end of the trial, the bracken cover consisted of fronds some 5 in (130 mm) tall at a frequency around six per square yard (7 per m²). Counts in 1957—after one year's recovery—showed that the bracken was beginning to regenerate both in height and density. The rate of recovery is important, not only botanically but financially; the slower the rate, the longer before a maintenance cut is required. Where bracken cover was sparse, there was a typical *Festuca/Agrostis* sward with patches of sweet vernal grass (*Anthoxanthum odoratum*) and wild white clover (*Trifolium repens*) commonly present. Where the canopy was dense, there was either no herbage present or patches of creeping soft grass (*Holcus mollis*). As the bracken was reduced, nettles and thistles appeared in places. However, with successive treatments, these weeds and the creeping soft grass were gradually replaced by *Festuca/Agrostis* spp. This replacement of weeds and poor grass by acceptable grazing species on bare earth sites, without any other treatment, was very encouraging.

Twenty years ago, economic appraisals—as distinct from simply establishing the costs—of various long-term improvements in agriculture were rare. The jargon of cost/benefit analysis was not yet heard in the land! The cost of treatment and the botanical aspects of frond reduction are capable of accurate measurement but, in contrast, an assessment of the sward improvement in husbandry and monetary terms is a much more complex task. However these trials, monitored over the mid-fifties, provided a good opportunity for moving forward from a well-documented base. The financial benefits of bracken control can arise in several ways, all stemming from the improved nutritional status of the sward and its *exploitation* at key times of the year:

(*a*) An increase in quality of the lambs (but no increase in numbers).
(*b*) An increase in lamb numbers (i.e. a higher lambing percentage).
(*c*) A combination of both.
(*d*) An increase in breeding ewes (and possibly in quality over time).
(*e*) A reduction in death rate of ewes (of least significance in practise).

These avenues of benefit are not mutually exclusive, but the kind and degree of response depends on many factors, not least of which is the predetermined role that the treated area is to play in the overall management of the hill. For example, on one of the farms in the Perthshire trials, the farmer's objective was to increase the overall quality of his pure Blackface flock (1080 ewes) at the existing rate of stocking 2·75 acres/ewe (1 ha). The cutting was done over 135 acres (55 ha) on the low-end of the hill—approximately 1000 acres (400 ha) in extent and separated from the higher land by a fence. This was a valuable grazing area for the whole sheep stock at certain times of the year. In a hard winter the ewes were moved down to this area; the lambing was carried out there and, after weaning, lambs were kept on the low hill until sale time or going off to wintering on 1st October. With this pattern of flock movement, and bearing in mind the ecological preferences of the bracken plant, the value of the treated area—13·5% of the low end—would be much higher than indicated by its actual size in acres.

The total cost (net of 50% grant) of the four-year programme (1952–55) was £210 or £1·55 per acre (£3·87/ha). All concerned were of the opinion that the benefit would probably last at least ten years. Thus, the average minimum improvement required to cover this cost would be £21 per annum. Given the level of performance and quality of the flock, the minimum improvement needed in terms of quality of lamb (price) was 11p per head per annum assuming, very conservatively, that only 25% of the lambs benefited; alternatively, in terms of extra numbers, 80 lambs or eight per annum. Full details of all sheep prices and numbers were kept from 1952 to 1957. The former were adjusted for seasonal variation, using indices based on the auction market at Perth; the latter, using indices based on surrounding hill farms where no bracken cutting or other forms of land improvement were taking place. The analysis confirmed the farmer's visual judgement that improvement had taken place in both quality and quantity. By the end of 1956 the cumulative increase in lamb numbers (93) alone was more than sufficient to cover the total cost of the treatment. In 1957 the number was a further 85 above the trend expectation.

Improvement in quality, as reflected in price at market, was slower to come. For store wedder lambs, there was no significant improvement relative to Perth market until 1955, when there was a rise of 50p; 1956, 27p; 1957, £1·25. These were the years when the effect of the cutting programme was at a maximum. A previous investigation had shown a similar pattern with the improvement lasting, but at a declining rate, for several years after the cessation of treatment. The size of the ewe flock, as a matter of policy, was kept constant. The better lamb crops permitted greater selection of ewe lamb replacements, and more rigorous culling of cast ewes. Such a policy is bound to have a beneficial effect on the productivity of a sheep stock over time. Even discounting any financial benefit stemming directly from the ewe flock, it was clear that the degree of improvement arising mainly from bracken control was such that by 1956 the cost of the treatment was more than adequately met. With at least a further five years to run before recutting was necessary, there can be little doubt that bracken control was a very worth-while economic exercise on this farm. That many farmers in the decade of the fifties were of the same opinion can be interpreted from figure 4.5.

A botanical and economic survey

At the suggestion of the Agricultural Research Council, a botanical and economic survey of bracken cutting on West of Scotland farms was undertaken in 1953. Some sixty farms were visited. The total area of bracken involved in a season was around 9500 acres (3800 ha) of which over 80% was cut by contractors. Scythe cutting was by far the most common method of control. The main reasons for this were threefold: topography, the scarcity of labour on farms, and the more urgent tasks of sheep handlings and low-ground work clashing with the best time for cutting bracken. Although frond counts from 52 areas showed considerable variations between sites, over four seasons the average reduction in height and density was 75% and 50% respectively. Only four (7%) of the farmers in the survey had applied any manurial follow-up on the treated areas. The application of two tons of lime per acre appeared to have beneficial effects on the sward.

Over the three seasons 1950 to 1953, the average annual *gross* cost of cutting one acre twice per season was:

	per acre	per hectare
with self-propelled machine	£0·82	£2·05
with tractor outfits	£0·82	£2·05
by contract scythe	£1·25	£3·09
by contract machine	£1·32	£3·30

Receipt of the bracken-cutting grant halved the cost to the farmer. In the early fifties a three-year programme of bracken control by scythe was costing around £1·80 to £2·00 net per acre. Where a farmer used his own tractor-operated machine, the equivalent figures were £1·00 to £1·50. At that time bracken cutting was regarded as an expensive but not necessarily uneconomic operation. Today, the scythe with its low rate of work—an acre per day—has been overtaken by high labour costs and is completely uneconomic. For the tractor-operated machine the above programme would, at 1974 prices, cost in the region of £5 to £6 net. As will be argued later, however, there is still a role for this type of machine.

The majority of farmers in the survey were of the opinion that bracken control was financially worth while, indeed essential in some cases. This was not so much with a view to increasing the stock-carrying capacity of the grazing in the first instance—although on a number of farms this was achieved—but rather to maintain the present position or in cases of bad infestation to prevent an ultimate decrease. When analysed on this basis, 48 farms were maintaining current flock numbers and benefiting through improved production per ewe. On six farms, bracken cutting led directly to an increase in flock numbers. In those instances where case studies were possible, it was obvious that bracken control was very worth while financially. On the remaining six, the extent and rate of spread of bracken was such that either the bracken had to be brought under control, or the number of ewes reduced. Such a reduction is an action of last resort on a hill farm. It was clear that the "premium" paid for bracken control was financially prudent in both the short and long term.

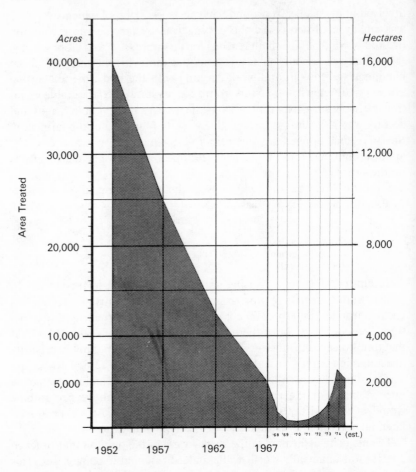

Figure 4.5 Trend in bracken areas treated under official schemes (figures from D.A.F.S. Annual Reports, H.M.S.O.).

Reasons for decline in control

Government assistance towards the control of this serious weed problem has been in operation in various forms since 1936. Under the present scheme, introduced in 1941, a 50% grant is paid for approved programmes of double cutting in a season, and normally for not longer than three seasons on the same area. The annual statistics of the scheme make interesting, if somewhat depressing, reading. Even in the peak year of 1952, the acreage treated was less than 10% of the national total, and in the space of 20 years it fell from 40,000 acres (16,000 ha) to virtually zero in

1971. Although the statistics do not separately distinguish acreages treated by mechanical means and those by herbicide—first approved for a 50% grant in 1972—it is fairly certain that the upturn in the curve from 1972 onwards largely represents new methods of chemical control applied in the main by helicopter. The reasons for the virtual cessation of bracken cutting are predominantly economic (see Table 4.3 on page 113). A general decline in the profitability of the industry leads inevitably to a shortage of capital for long-term projects of improvement. In such a situation priority decisions become crucial. The concurrent and dramatic increase in beef cows must have siphoned off a large share of available finance. Even where capital was not a limiting factor, the steep rise in costs, particularly for scythe work, caused a marked deterioration in the relationship between costs and sheep prices. Also, the decline in the labour force continued over the years. To a minor extent, psychological factors may have played a part, particularly in the late sixties when there was considerable interest and speculation about the prospect of a suitable spray which would eradicate bracken in one operation. Some farmers did defer action on that account.

Chemical control

On arable crops and lowland pastures the control of weeds by selective chemicals is one of the modern success stories of agriculture. Unfortunately, this advance has not been matched on the hills. The reason for the difference in the rate of progress is again economic, bearing in mind the relative values of output per acre from low ground and hill country. Technically, the chemical approach is potentially more fruitful than conventional defoliation methods. A selective herbicide spray which is capable of being translocated into the rhizome system is getting to the heart of the problem! Recent field research work, however, with asulam—the first and as yet the only herbicide to be officially approved for grant purposes— shows little visual evidence of adequate translocation *within* the relatively inert rhizome system. In practical terms, aerial spraying overcomes two major limiting factors to mechanical treatment, namely, topography and lack of labour. Also, a worth-while acreage can be done in hours rather than days. Experience in Scotland with asulam has shown that from mid-July to mid-August is the most effective period for application. At a rate of 4 lb active ingredient per acre (4·5 kg/ha) asulam has given very satisfactory levels of frond reduction (85%–98%) in the following season. This order of reduction in density is significantly higher than that achieved by a three-year cutting programme. Unfortunately, however, it is not an eradicant, and botanists involved in field trials are agreed that regeneration of fronds can be at a rate of 10% or more per annum. Although only time will tell, it would seem that the interval before further treatment is required will, except in some exceptional cases, be no longer than that with conventional cutting over three seasons. The question of relative costs remains.

Machine or chemical?

In 1974 a common quotation for aerial spraying by helicopter was £15 per acre (£37/ha) gross. It is a statutory provision of the bracken spraying scheme that, to qualify for a 50% grant, the area sprayed must be part of a more extensive programme of hill-land improvement. The *minimum* follow-up treatment in areas where access is difficult would be 3 cwt of ground mineral phosphate per acre (£5). If the provision were met, the net cost of the herbicide would be £7·50 per acre. The comparable cost of a three-year programme, ending in 1974, of cutting by a farmer's own tractor-mounted machine would be in the region of £5 to £6. Depreciation on the machine is included, but not on the tractor, as it is part of the existing fixed costs of the farm. Wages are included but, if the driver were a regular employee, the overall wages bill would not be altered. These two items make up 75% to 80% of the cost, provided that no major mishap befalls the outfit. As well as being cheaper in full-cost terms, the machine method is more advantageous in terms of cash flow. A hundred acres (40 ha) of bracken sprayed by helicopter will require £750 in cash in one season (plus £500 minimum for fertilizer) whereas £350 (est.) will be required to purchase the machine in the first year and the operating costs of the programme will be spread over three years.

Whither now?

On the basis of the evidence available since the war, there can be little doubt that the vast majority of farmers did not consider the extra response to lime or fertilizers either necessary in practice or worth while financially. Considering the magnitude of the problem, it seems a pity that such a proviso should be applied in *every case* of chemical control. In effect, it must mean that large areas of bracken, formerly cut by contract scythe, will be left untreated. Although one can spray and forego the grant, £15 per acre would seem rather imprudent! A discretionary system, depending on the degree of infestation, location, etc., would have been more satisfactory. Undoubtedly, the synchronizing of bracken control with a wider programme of hill land improvement is a welcome advance. In areas of dense bracken, fertilizer and reseeding will often be necessary if a useful sward is to be quickly established. For lighter canopies, however, this is not so on past evidence. A more flexible system of grant aid for chemical spraying, which is an undoubted breakthrough in methodology if not in economics, could bring under control thousands of acres of bracken presently ignored.

In the short term, the outlook for a significant reduction in the national stand of 400,000 acres is bleak. Experience over a quarter of a century leaves the impression that no *major* impact will be made until an effective eradicant is found. The whole financial equation would then be altered. On areas of heavy infestation, the money spent on a once-and-for-all spray plus sward improvement would be akin to buying extra acres at well below the current price of hill land. In the meantime, the acreage tackled will depend heavily on the overall state of the hill sheep industry. When the cost/price relationship improves and capital is again available, bracken control either by mechanical or chemical means will move much higher up the scale of priorities. Those farmers who were enthusiastic in the past know, as do the foresters, that the bracken fern is a reliable indicator of potentially the best areas of the hill.

FURTHER READING (Part 1)

John Eadie (1971), "Hill Pastoral Resources and Sheep Production", *Proc. Nutrition Soc.*, **30**.
R. W. Gloyne (1968), "Some Climatic Influences affecting Hill Land Productivity", *Hill Land Productivity*, edit. I. V. Hunt, Occasional Symposium No. 4, British Grassland Society.
A. McLeod (1972), "The Hill Farmer's Viewpoint", Colloquium Proc. No. 3, Hill Pasture Improvement and its Economic Utilisation, Edinburgh, The Potassium Institute Ltd.
I. A. Nicholson, D. C. Currie, I. S. Paterson and J. B. McCreath (1968), "Hill Grazing Management and Increased Production", *Scottish Agriculture*, **47**, H.M.S.O.
A. J. F. Russel (1971), "Relationships Between Energy Intake and Productivity in Hill Sheep", *Proc. Nutrition Soc.*, **30**.
H. Whitby (1970), "Some Developments in Scottish Farming Since the War", *Jour. Agric. Economics*, XXI, No. 1.

Edit. Joy Tivy (1973), *The Organic Resources of Scotland*, Oliver and Boyd, Edinburgh.

Readers particularly interested in the research aspects should refer to the triennial reports published by the Hill Farming Research Organisation, Bush Estate, Penicuik, Midlothian.

FURTHER READING (Part 2)

Bracken Control
Joan Mitchell (1973), "The Bracken Problem", in *The Organic Resources of Scotland* (ed. Joy Tivy), Oliver and Boyd, Edinburgh.

G. F. Hendry (1958), "The Size of Scotland's Bracken Problem", *Scottish Agricultural Economics*, Vol. IX, H.M.S.O.

J. B. McCreath and J. D. Forrest (1958), "Bracken Control Machinery Trials", Res. Bull. No. 24 W.S. Agric. Coll.

A. D. McKelvie and E. B. Scragg (1973), "The Control of Bracken by Asulam", *Scottish Agriculture*, **51**, H.M.S.O.

D. J. Martin (1974), "Control of Bracken", Symposium on Biology of Bracken, Linnean Soc., London. (In press.)

Leslie Rymer (1974), "History of Bracken", Symposium on Biology of Bracken, Linnean Soc., London. (In press.)

CHAPTER FIVE

RECLAMATION OF THE URBAN ENVIRONMENT

NINIAN JOHNSTON

Introduction

The movement to reclaim the urban environment of our cities is a comparatively new phenomenon. It may be seen as an attempt to recreate physical and social environments which have fallen into decay following changes in the economic and industrial base of society— changes exacerbated by a very fast rate of physical growth. These areas of decay can be directly related to the aftermath of the Industrial Revolution in Western Europe. Britain has arguably the largest problem in this respect, since it was the first to be extensively developed as an industrial nation.

While the industrialized cities were developing, attempts were being made to deal with the chaotic results of rapid and uncontrolled growth. The Public Health Acts and Model Building Bye-laws introduced in Britain in the last century moderated the very worst aspects of urban deprivation, but did little to change significantly the quality of life. The same is true of the early planning legislation introduced in Europe (notably Germany) at about the same time. A fundamental change in *suburban* environments was effected by forward-looking movements such as the philanthropic housing developments sponsored by Leverhulme and the Cadburys, and Ebenezer Howard's Garden City plans. But there were few attempts to apply these ideas to reshaping and improving decaying inner areas of cities in a comprehensive way. Thus the problems created in the obsolete sub-central environs of our Victorian towns and cities are with us today.

Contemporary reclamation seeks to construct new environments and communities as well as new buildings. While controlled and coordinated planning maintains the standards applied to new towns, the associated difficulties are considerable when compared to new development on a virgin site. The logistics are complex; completion time seems inordinately long. There has been some success in the 20 or so years in which meaningful urban renewal has been attempted, but such efforts have not been entirely satisfactory.

The city of Glasgow is uniquely placed to give a dramatic illustration of the problems of urban reclamation. In qualitative terms, the areas of obsolescence in Glasgow are not significantly worse than in other cities of comparable size, such as Birmingham, Manchester or Liverpool. The main difference lies in the way in which the other major cities of Britain have managed to adapt and diversify within a twentieth-century economy. The economic decline of Glasgow since the end of the nineteenth century has been followed by no such revival. In many ways the city is a waste product of a redundant economy. The inertia following the decline of heavy industry has allowed urban decay to spread until it is now greater than in any other city in Britain. To compound the problem, a weakened local economy has created severe difficulties in financing a programme of urban renewal. Notwithstanding the obstacles, Glasgow has courageously undertaken environmental reclamation on a larger scale than any other British city.

In outlining the process of environmental recovery in Glasgow, the Gorbals district will be taken as a case in point. This small area of the city has passed into urban mythology as a by-word for the worst evils of the slum. In common with other myths, the actuality has been somewhat distorted, but it is true that the Gorbals did contain some of the worst housing conditions in Glasgow. For that reason, and in an effort to improve the city's image, part of the Gorbals was chosen as the first area to be redeveloped in Glasgow's post-war urban renewal programme. The redevelopment is now almost complete, having taken place over a period of 17 years. This makes it possible to review the entire process of one of the first attempts to reclaim the urban environment in this country, and to compare it with the changed attitudes and methods used today.

The reshaping of this area of Glasgow cannot be seen as an isolated event initiated in 1957. A synoptic view of the evolution of urban redevelopment in this country is vital to the understanding of the Gorbals story.

The main part of this chapter has therefore been arranged into three sections: the first gives a brief historical outline of developments in Britain from the mid-nineteenth century until the reconstruction legislation of the post World War II era and an account of Glasgow's particular problems throughout this period.

The second section deals with the redevelopment of the Gorbals in a city-wide and local context. It also describes the procedures used to set in motion the process of redevelopment.

The third section attempts to gauge the success of the new Gorbals. The recent changes in attitude and philosophy regarding the process of urban redevelopment in Glasgow since its inception in the late 1950s are also discussed.

Planning in Britain 1850–1950

The growth in the economy of Britain in the nineteenth century made it one of the most prosperous nations of the world. But that prosperity was bought at a fearful price, for which we are still paying at a time when our economy is declining. Most of us have some notion of the dreadful conditions which existed in the industrial towns of Victorian Britain. The chroniclers of that time such as Chadwick and Engels, the information produced by each National Census since 1801, and the reports of government inquiries present the cold statistics. What is perhaps difficult for us to appreciate is the extent of human suffering which accompanied them. It is beyond the scope of this chapter to dwell on this aspect. It is our concern to investigate what action was taken to alleviate these conditions and to outline the frustrations and advances occasioned by political, economic and social pressures which evolved into the situation where reclamation of the urban environment became possible.

Conditions in a modern industrial city cannot be compared to those of Victorian Britain, although many aspects of the nineteenth-century slum have continued well into the twentieth century. The legislation of the nineteenth century gradually disposed of the very worst problems of the industrial environment. Epidemic and contagious diseases, such as cholera and typhus, were controlled. Pure water supplies were introduced, as were better sanitary facilities, and the disposal of sewage and refuse. The building bye-laws improved the construction of dwellings, particularly with regard to fire risk and proper ventilation. These measures can be seen as preventive rather than constructive in nature.

Other aspects of the intolerable conditions brought about by the Industrial Revolution remain in the second half of the twentieth century. Large areas of residential development, badly built to very high densities, have been allowed to fall into decay. Overcrowding in minute living areas, with consequent lack of privacy, continues. Lack of proper plan making and control has led to acres of drab featureless housing being developed without adequate facilities for play or recreation, in which residential and industrial land uses have been juxtaposed without regard to health or visual amenity. These are the conditions which urban redevelopment seeks to transform.

The major legislation to improve the urban environment could broadly be described in chronological order as the Health Acts, the Housing Acts and the Planning Acts. Since the end of the First World War, the Housing and Planning Acts have played an inter-related role.

Housing legislation

Before 1875 the powers of local authorities to initiate projects for areas of slum clearance were severely restricted. Most legislation in this respect met with considerable opposition before it was enacted. Interference by central and local government was seen as an infringement of private liberty and free enterprise. Even the major Health Acts were weakened in their detailed legislation, and in many areas local authorities found it impossible to enforce improvement. Any scheme for local improvement of the physical environment had to be approved by Parliament, where it often encountered strong opposition. Local Acts of Parliament for specific projects were sought by local authorities and private companies. The powers granted under these Acts were used mainly for private railway development or by city councils wishing to make civic improvements, such as the widening or formation of roads.

Many of the worst areas of decay occurred close to city centres, and commercial and industrial expansion often surrounded isolated pockets of high-density slum land. In clearing these areas for "civic improvement", the municipalities were not entirely altruistic. These slums were often seen as an embarrassing stigma and a danger to public health. The Victorian municipal conscience was salved by their demolition, but there was generally no scheme for re-housing, and the cheap slum land was often used for commercial exploitation or for public works. The object was rather to get rid of a nuisance than to act positively to improve living conditions.

Various Acts of Parliament from 1868 to 1885 gave increased scope for action by municipalities, but in detail these Acts had similar weaknesses to the earlier Health Acts; very little was achieved. The Housing of the Working Classes Act of 1890 brought together many of the features of the previous legislation, and gave local authorities increased powers. The main provision of the Act was that for the first time local authorities were enabled to declare improvement schemes on a reasonable scale, to acquire land by compulsory purchase, and to build houses for the working class.

The Housing and Town Planning Act of 1909 for the first time made it a *duty* for a local authority to carry out inspections to ascertain the "fitness" of houses, to impose closing orders where necessary, and to demolish such buildings, and to recover costs. A significant aspect of the Act was that it also enabled local authorities to prepare town planning schemes. This was perhaps the first occasion that the proper planning of towns was admitted as being relevant by central government.

Despite the widened scope given to local authorities under this legislation, there was no provision made to link slum clearance and new housing with the comprehensive planning of the inner areas of cities. This was partly due to the weakness of existing legislation, and partly to the ease of developing green-field sites on the periphery of built-up areas. This trend was influenced by the garden suburb movement, which was in vogue just before and after the Great War. The fundamental weakness of this Act, and of nineteenth-century legislation in general, was that, although extensive *authority* was given to municipalities in respect of public health, slum clearance and house building, there was no statutory *obligation* to initiate improvement.

Most important of all, there was no financial assistance available from central government. The local rates were the only source of funds for redevelopment and, in practice, political opposition often made this virtually impossible. In addition, each individual scheme required parliamentary approval, and this often created more frustration and delay. Only the large cities of Glasgow, Birmingham and Liverpool made any real progress, and this was on a limited scale under special "city acts". The lack of activity by local authorities was underlined by a Royal Commission on Housing in Scotland in 1917. The Commission observed that, from 1890 to 1913, only 3484 families (0·33% of the total) had been rehoused by local authorities. Most of these had been rehoused in Glasgow. The Commission estimated that at the end of the Great War some 236,000 houses were required, of which over 121,000 were "immediately necessary".

Planning legislation

The catharsis of social and political change brought about by the First World War was reflected in the post-war Housing and Planning legislation. The Housing and Town Planning Act of 1919 laid the groundwork for the main housing and planning legislation of the inter-war years. For the first time, local authorities were *required* to provide adequate housing for the urban population, and were to be given financial assistance from central government. With reference to town planning, all municipalities with populations of 20,000 and above were required to prepare simplified town planning schemes for any new development carried out under the Act. These planning schemes were required to include:

   (i) the limitations of building densities per acre;
   (ii) the defining of that portion of the site area of a dwelling house to be covered with buildings;
   (iii) the character of buildings;
   (iv) the lines of proposed arterial roads and the associated building lines;
   (v) the provision of open spaces.

Other provisions of the Act aimed at simplifying the procedure of compulsory acquisition, and at producing a more realistic basis for calculating compensation. In addition, the Housing Manual of 1919, which was produced primarily as a guide for local authorities, made recommendations on such matters as site planning, standards of accommodation, densities and design criteria. Although the 1919 Act made considerable advances in the provision of new housing, laid out to reasonable standards, and made exchequer funds available for the purpose, there was generally scant attention paid to the problems of the older inner areas of cities. The policy of "Homes fit for Heroes" was relentlessly pursued. In the single-minded devotion to providing housing at all costs, the spirit of the planning philosophy contained in the 1919 Act was largely neglected; local authorities found it less complicated and cheaper to develop "green field" sites on the edges of towns, and large areas of monotonous suburban development were quickly constructed. The social needs of communities, such as schools, adequate shopping provision, libraries, churches, public houses, etc., followed much later.

Despite the fact that a subsidy for slum clearance had been available since 1923, there was very little action on this front. The economic slump of the 1930s saw a contraction of new house building, aided by the withdrawal of the housing subsidy in 1934. In the period from 1919 to 1934, some 100,500 houses had been built in Scotland. This did not even meet the requirement of 121,000 houses of "immediate need" put forward by the Royal Commission in 1917. The Housing Acts of the 1930s were the results of muddled policies as between new housing and slum clearance, and were subject to considerable economic and political pressures.

The Housing Act of 1930 gave subsidies both for slum clearance and rehousing, with stress laid on the latter, whilst the 1933 Act concentrated almost exclusively on slum clearance. The 1935 Act emphasized overcrowding rather than slum clearance as such. A significant section of this Act put forward a policy with regard to the redevelopment of areas of slum housing (the "reconstruction" areas). This was the first attempt to redevelop decayed inner city housing as new environments.

Despite the efforts of both government and local authorities since 1919 to create a totally new concept in the housing of the working population, and to create in cities humane, healthy and modern environments, success was far off. During the economic depression of the 1930s, large numbers of houses which would have been determined "fit" previously, had fallen into decay due to lack of proper maintenance and control of the standards of private rented accommodation. The raising of standards of "fitness", e.g. in overcrowding, had compounded the problem. In 1944 the Scottish Housing Advisory Committee estimated that there was a basic need for at least 500,000 houses, double the figure estimated by the Royal Commission in 1917.

Philosophy of reconstruction

It is perhaps strange that Britain's "great leap forward" in national planning strategy was stimulated when the country was at war. The need to reconstruct the blitzed areas of cities was evident but, more than this, there appears to have been a national concern that the post-war reconstruction of the country would be based for the first time on social justice tempered with equity. The considerable energy devoted to this task by the war-time government culminated in several major Reports and national planning Acts, which were to influence profoundly the development of urban areas for a generation.

For some time before the war there had been a growing awareness that the housing and planning legislation of the 1930s was inadequate to deal with the situation in many of our cities. The sprawling suburbs of the inter-war years presented difficulties of crisis proportions in terms of traffic and transportation, and the relationship between home and work. The haphazard layout of the Victorian city centres could not cope with the growing congestion of the twentieth century. There was also concern with the problems generated by unemployment, particularly in the north of England and in Scotland, and the growing attraction of industry and population to London and the South East. Another factor which tended to frustrate development in the inter-war period was the problem associated with compensation and betterment in respect of the public control of the use of land. The Barlow Report (1940) and the Uthwatt Report (1941) made recommendations which in large measure overcame the problems outlined above. The recommendations contained in these Reports formed the basis for much of the reconstruction legislation passed between 1943 and 1947.

There were three main recommendations contained in the Barlow Report: (1) there should be a national planning authority to oversee and integrate regional planning objectives; (2) obsolete and overburdened urban areas should be redeveloped, and their industries and populations dispersed; (3) there should be a balance of industrial development throughout all areas of Britain. These recommendations were embodied in the Distribution of Industry Act (1945) and the New Towns Act (1946).

The main recommendations of the Uthwatt Report were: that control over the development of land should be vested in local authorities; that the "reconstruction areas" (of the 1935 Housing Act) should be redefined; that the planning of these areas, together with replacement due to war damage, should be carried out on a comprehensive basis; and that consequent redevelopment schemes should form part of the long-term planning strategies for urban areas. In the matter of compensation and betterment, it was suggested that the State should have development rights on all land outside built-up areas, and it was recommended that areas of developed land should be compulsorily acquired for the planning and development of the areas of reconstruction and war damage. The main aim of the Report in respect of the latter was to stabilize the value of land, in order that post-war reconstruction could be realistically carried out.

With government acceptance of the philosophy behind the Barlow and Uthwatt reports, it was obvious that considerable powers would be devolved on local authorities. The legislation came in the 1944 Planning Act. Sweeping powers were indeed given to local authorities to enable the development of the areas of reconstruction and war damage, and to this end the process of compulsory acquisition was streamlined. In a sense this Act was a stop-gap measure. The question of the relationship between the redevelopment areas and the planning and control of development in urban areas as a whole had yet to be resolved. This was achieved in the 1947 Planning Act, which was to be the principal instrument in planning legislation until the late 1960s.

The 1947 Act embodied and extended many of the provisions of the 1944 Act. The main provisions were:

1. All planning authorities were required to prepare a Development Plan for all land under their control, this plan to be revised every five years. Plan reviews and amendments would be subject to ministerial approval and public inquiry. The Development Plan would show (*a*) the manner in which all land is to be used whether by development or otherwise, and (*b*) the stages by which development will be carried out.

2. *All* development, whether carried out by a local authority or a private developer, would be subject to the granting of planning permission by the planning authority.

3. The likely areas for compulsory purchase were to be indicated on the Development Plan.

4. The areas of "reconstruction" were redefined as Comprehensive Development Areas,

and these could be designated for compulsory purchase. A Comprehensive Development Area (CDA) was defined as:

any area which, in the opinion of the local planning authority, could be developed as a whole for

(a) dealing satisfactorily with extensive war damage or conditions of bad layout or obsolete development;

(b) relocating population or industry, or replacing open space in the course of development or redevelopment of another area;

(c) achieving any other purpose specified in the Development Plan.

In addition, exchequer grants were to be made available for the redevelopment of areas other than those suffering war damage. It was under this legislation that the comprehensive redevelopment of the Gorbals was undertaken. Unfortunately, as with the 1919 Act, the initiative and drive of the planning legislation gave way to the hard realities of the housing shortage. As in the 1920s, the early 1950s saw a concentration of new house building on the peripheries of cities. There was a similar lack of social amenities, such as shops, schools and churches. Although the government target figure of 300,000 houses per year for Britain was fulfilled, it left in its wake problems in the large suburban housing estates which, in the case of Glasgow, have not entirely been resolved. The return to quality rather than quantity did not occur until the mid-1950s, when there was fresh consideration of slum clearance and the redevelopment of inner city areas. By this time the financial stringencies of the immediate post-war period had given way to a much more buoyant economy.

The situation in Glasgow

As suggested in the Introduction, Glasgow's economy has been in a state of inertia since the turn of the century. Two world wars compounded the situation, for they artificially prolonged the life of the city's heavy-industry base. The collapse of the economy was thus more real than apparent. Failure, to find an alternative to heavy industry has continued the economic decline up to the present. Unemployment in Glasgow has been considerably higher than the national average for many years.* In addition, many of the new industries which have been established in West Central Scotland under government incentive schemes have been attracted to the New Towns and other areas round the City, where the environment is more attractive, where a high percentage of the workforce is skilled, and where the rates burden is much less than in Glasgow.

It is partly for these reasons that Glasgow is struggling to create a fundamental restructuring of its environment. The present city policies

* During the last 15 years unemployment has been approximately twice the national average.

with regard to the development of the city centre, the proposed Highway Plan with the associated improvements in public transport, and the redevelopment areas have for some time been seen as necessary components in changing the city's image and improving its ability to function efficiently as a modern city with an attractive environment.

It is hoped that, by achieving this aim, Glasgow will be able to compete more effectively with other more fortunate areas, and to attract new industry and employment. Underlying this aim, there is a goal which can be described as a basic desire to improve the quality of the social and physical environment, and to bring about increased opportunities for a better lifestyle for the city's population. In the implementation of these policies, the objectives of the Corporation of Glasgow have been seen in terms of tackling physical problems.

Recently the city has come under considerable criticism for this unilateral approach. Such attacks are not, however, entirely justified because; (1) it is often not appreciated that the scale and intensity of the physical problem is greater than in any other British city of comparable size, and (2) with a weak local economy, great reliance has been placed on the participatory role of government agencies (notably the Scottish Development Department) and on special government subsidies. These subsidies have inevitably concentrated on physical development.

Seen in this light, criticism should be more correctly aimed at the policies of central government. The preoccupation with physical problems has for decades been directed towards the two topics of an inadequate housing stock and escalating slum conditions. As stated earlier, the phenomenally rapid growth of industrial cities in the last century was one of the factors in the basic creation of bad housing and slums. In this respect Glasgow was no exception. Figures 5.1 and 5.2 illustrate the growth of both the city and the population between 1801 and 1938. At the census of 1801 the city's population was 77,000; by 1841 the population had trebled, and by 1891 it was double the 1841 figure. Although the city boundaries had been extended from time to time (figure 5.1), there was always an increased demand for building land over the available supply.

The Scottish tradition of building houses in tenements was ideally suited to overcome the shortage of land for development. This form of building gave rise to very high densities in many working class areas. Densities of from 450–700 people per acre were common, although the average density figure adopted by the Corporation today is 70–90 persons per acre. In the early period of development (1841–1861) these high densities, together with considerable overcrowding, created appalling living conditions. An article in a contemporary journal (*The Artizan*, 1843) gives the following account of conditions in Glasgow:

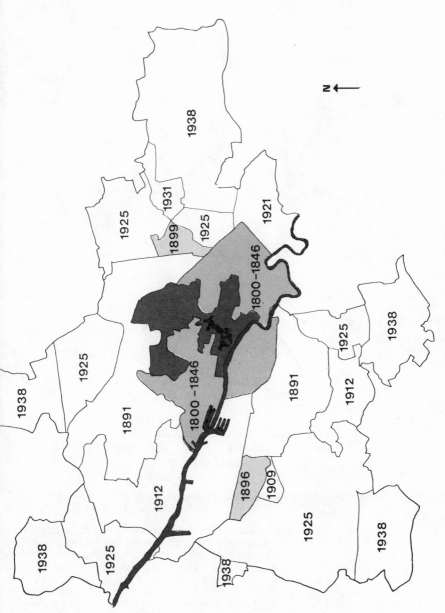

Figure 5.1 City expansion in Glasgow (not to scale).

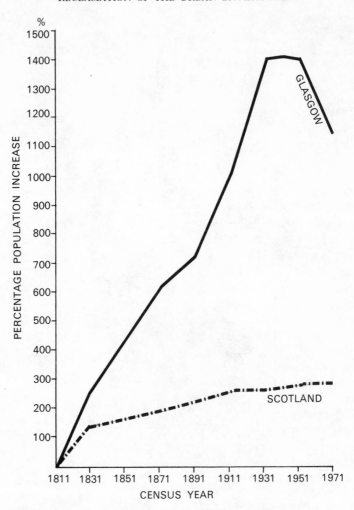

FIGURE 5.2   Comparative population increase in Glasgow and Scotland (1811–1971).

The population in 1840 was estimated at 282,000, of whom about 70% belong to the working classes, 50,000 of whom are Irish. Glasgow has its fine airy healthy quarters . . . but it has many others which, in abject wretchedness, exceed the lowest purlieus of St. Giles or Whitechapel, the Liberties of Dublin or the wynds of Edinburgh. Such localities exist most abundantly in the heart of the city . . . endless labyrinths of narrow lanes or wynds, into which at almost every step debouch courts or closes formed by old, ill-ventilated, towering houses crumbling to decay, destitute of water and crowded with inhabitants comprising three or four families (perhaps twenty persons) on each flat, and sometimes each flat let out for lodgings that confine—we dare not say accommodate—from fifteen to twenty persons in a single room. These districts are occupied by the poorest, most depraved, and most worthless portion of the population, and they may be considered as the fruitful source of those pestilential fevers which thence spread their destructive ravages over the whole of Glasgow. . . .

An official inquiry (Symonds, 1839) into the condition of handloom weavers described the slums of Glasgow:

I have seen human degradation in some of its worst phases, both in England and abroad, but I can advisedly say that I did not believe until I visited the wynds of Glasgow that so large an amount of filth, crime, misery and disease existed in one spot in any civilised country . . . In the lower lodging houses, ten, twelve and sometimes twenty persons of both sexes and all ages sleep promiscuously on the floor in different degrees of nakedness. These places are generally, as regards dirt, damp and decay, such as no person of common humanity to animals would stable his horse in.

The conditions were somewhat relieved by the granting by Parliament of the City Improvement Act in 1866 and a similar Act in 1897. Under these Acts, some 88 acres of the worst slums in an around the city centre were improved in the period before the Great War. During this period the Corporation had built some 3300 houses, 5 lodging houses, and over 560 shops and business premises. In the period from 1858 to 1900 it is estimated that over 100,000 houses were built in the city. In the inter-war period, under various Housing Acts, Glasgow Corporation had built more than 110,000 houses and had closed 18,000 as "unfit": 15,000 of these had been demolished in slum-clearance programmes. Despite this considerable housing programme, a survey made by the city's Medical Officer of Health in 1935 revealed that over 82,000 people were living in overcrowded conditions. In 1945 it was estimated (First Development Plan Survey Report, 1951) that at least 172,000 sub-standard houses would require to be demolished.

Most of the housing estates of the inter-war period had been erected on green-field sites on the outskirts of the city. Such was the speed of development that many of these remote suburbs lacked the supporting social amenities necessary for the development of new communities. This trend was mirrored in the post-war period when the philosophy was "houses at any cost". Many of the remaining areas on the fringe of the city as extended in 1938 were quickly eaten up by large housing estates, with the inevitable lack of amenities. By the mid-1950s the shortage of building land was acute, for the city could no longer extend its boundaries, surrounded as they were by ancient burghs intent on preserving their independence, by first-grade agricultural land and by mining development. There was also a national green-belt policy operated by Glasgow and the surrounding counties.

As outlined above, the necessity to build more houses in the post-1945 era was seen as a first priority. The immediate post-war housing developments had helped (in the period 1945–1953 some 30,000 houses had been built by the Corporation) but by the mid-1950s there were about 100,000 people on the Corporation's housing waiting list, and over half of the city's population still lived in the older Victorian tenemental areas in unsatisfactory housing conditions, some with average densities of 450 persons per acre.

Faced with a housing shortage, a large waiting list, and a lack of developable land, the Corporation turned its attention to the redevelopment of the inner areas. A report to the Housing and Planning Committees of the Corporation as early as 1953 had proposed three inner city areas for comprehensive redevelopment. By 1957 the magnitude of the redevelopment problem had become much more acute, and in that year the City Architect and Planning Officer submitted a report suggesting that, in order to achieve a realistic clearance and redevelopment programme, some twenty-nine comprehensive development areas (CDA) should be established throughout the city (see figure 5.3). These areas varied in size from 25 acres to 270 acres, and had populations ranging from 4000 to 40,000. There were in addition some 2500 industrial concerns. The report stressed that proper arrangements for the decanting of population outwith the city (overspill) was essential to the success of the programme:

It cannot be too strongly emphasised that the provision outwith the City of accommodation for the reception of Glasgow's overspill is the governing factor in all proposals made in this Report. Without this provision little or no redevelopment . . . can be undertaken.

The Corporation's view was that overspill should be kept to a minimum: this implied that densities in the new redevelopment areas would require to be as high as possible (the figure generally adopted was 150 persons per acre). Despite the adoption of high densities, it was estimated that around 60% of the existing populations would still require to be relocated outwith the City under overspill agreements. This involved the decanting of over 200,000 people in a programme phased over twenty years. Providing the overspill arrangements could be achieved, the report suggested that some 97,000 houses would be required to be cleared in the same twenty-year period up to 1980.

Fortunately for Glasgow's redevelopment programme, this situation had been foreseen some years before, both in the Barlow Report and in Abercrombie's Clyde Valley Regional Plan of 1946. Abercrombie had recognized the difficulty of restructuring the high-density urban areas of the region with the associated problem of decanting population on a large scale. He proposed, as part of the solution, the building of four new towns, together with the expansion of existing communities. Since the end of the war, Government initiative had followed similar lines. Under the New Towns Act 1946–59, two new towns were built just outside the

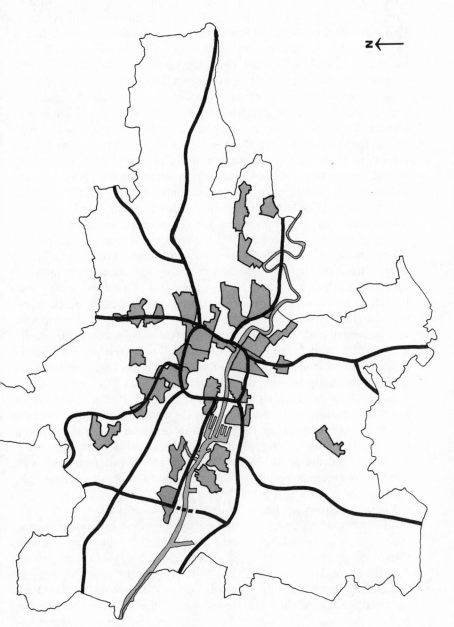

Figure 5.3 The principal highway network with the 29 comprehensive development areas (not to scale)

City at East Kilbride and Cumbernauld. Glenrothes was established in Fife. More recently Livingston in West Lothian, Irvine in Ayrshire, Erskine in Renfrewshire, and Stonehouse in Lanarkshire have been added to expand the programme. In addition to the new towns, under the provisions of the Housing and Town Development (Scotland) Act, 1957, agreements have been reached between Glasgow and over fifty local authorities throughout Scotland to provide 22,000 houses for overspill, the required balance to be achieved in the new towns. Under both schemes Glasgow nominates prospective families, and a grant is paid to the receiving authority. There was a similar scheme set up for the relocation of industry to ensure continuity of employment. One of the largest barriers to the redevelopment programme had been lifted with the establishment of these overspill arrangements.

From its inception, the Comprehensive Development Area Programme had further reaching implications for city-wide planning than simply the clearance of slum housing and the creation of modern attractively-planned residential areas. Each area, as the title implies, had to be planned comprehensively; i.e. it had to be reasonably self-sufficient in terms of support facilities for the new population. Areas of land use were zoned for activities such as commercial development, education, open space and industry. In this way it was hoped that the new areas of development would bring about a rationalization and updating of commercial activity (principally shopping) and would enable land to be released for modern industrial development in association with an improved highway network.

The relationship between the development of the CDAs and the City's Highway Plan has been significant. The Highway Plan was seen as an important instrument in dealing with: (1) growing congestion brought about by increased traffic; (2) facilitation of traffic and transportation movements within the city; (3) improved accessibility to the City from the region and the south. In this way Glasgow hoped to maintain its position as a regional employment centre, and to improve its trade links with the rest of the country.

Figure 5.4 shows the relationship of the inner-area CDAs to the city-centre ring road as delineated in the Highway Plan (a city-centre ring road appears in the first City Plan in 1946). Figure 5.3 shows the relationship of the proposed CDAs to the system of motorways and expressways detailed in the Highway Plan. The stage was set for redevelopment to proceed. This was officially acknowledged in the approval of the Quinquennial Review of the City Development Plan in 1960. The reader, however, should not be under the impression that the programme has developed smoothly in a continuous and integrated way. The time scale for the redevelopment of a CDA can be spread in phases over a period

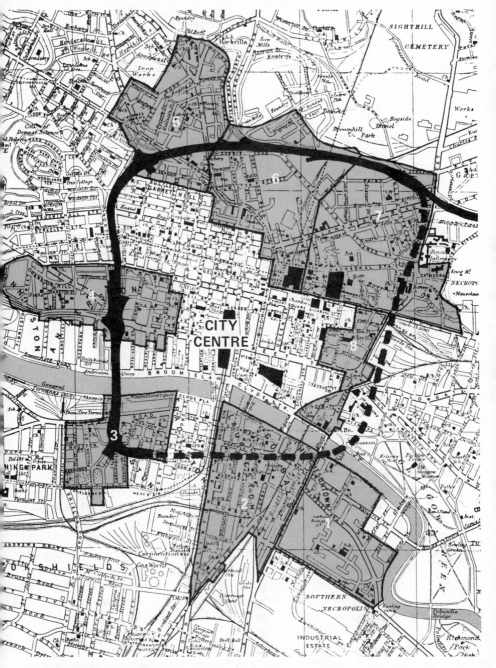

Figure 5.4 The original inner comprehensive development areas and the ring road.

1. Hutchesontown/Gorbals
2. Laurieston/Gorbals
3. Shields Road (Kinning Park)
4. Anderston
5. Woodside
6. Cowcaddens
7. Townhead
8. Glasgow Cross

Reproduced by permission of John Bartholomew & Son Limited

of up to twenty years, but the plan preparation and implementation of a single CDA, together with the legal difficulties associated with compulsory purchase and compensation, fully stretch the manpower resources of the Corporation. The result is that there are considerable time intervals between the approval of one CDA and another.

Of the nine CDAs which have the approval of the Corporation and the Secretary of State, the first was approved in 1957 and the most recent in 1973. Clearly the early hope of completing a considerable portion of the redevelopment programme by 1980 will not be realized. In addition, the entire redevelopment programme has been overtaken by events at a national level. In the intervening period between the setting up of the first CDA in the Gorbals in 1957 and the present, there has been a move away from the type of plan-making which was evident in the immediate post-war period. The shift away from what has been termed "determinist physical planning" has been reflected in recent planning and housing legislation (1969–1974). The implications of this change in attitude as it effects the CDA approach to redevelopment will be discussed at page 164. There is no doubt, however, that the CDA in Glasgow has brought about far-reaching changes in the physical and social environment of the City. We will now see how these changes came about in one area of the city—the Gorbals.

THE GORBALS STORY

Historical background

The area known today as the Gorbals is situated on the south bank of the River Clyde, less than a quarter of a mile from Glasgow Cross—the traditional centre of the city. Although close to the heart of the city, the area did not come under the jurisdiction of the Corporation until 1846. Until the end of the eighteenth century, the Gorbals consisted of about 47 acres of open fields, together with the two small villages of Bridgend (or Gorbals) and Little Govan in the east of the area (figure 5.5).

Towards the end of the eighteenth century there was a major expansion of the city centre on the north bank of the Clyde towards the west, where Glasgow's rising merchant class built a new well-planned residential development on high ground, upwind from the stench and disease of the overcrowded centre. The first major development south of the river took place in the Gorbals area between the old Glasgow Bridge and the Jamaica Bridge.

The development, which was undertaken by the brothers James and

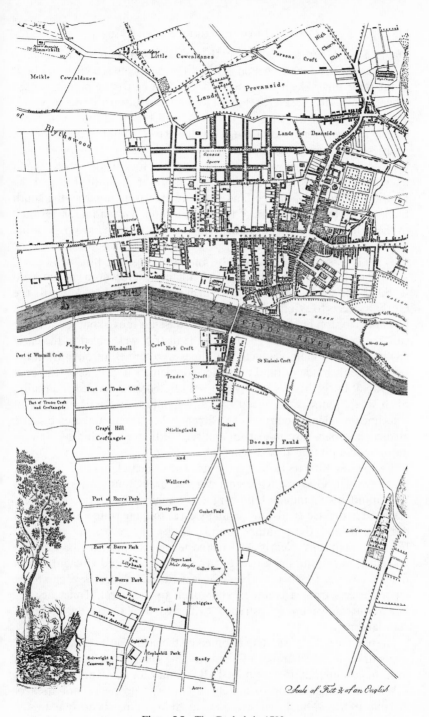

Figure 5.5 The Gorbals in 1782.

David Laurie, was conceived in the grand manner as a high-quality residential quarter which would rival Edinburgh's New Town, being built at the same time. The layout was to be "according to one plan or design whereby it was in a measure set apart for houses of a superior description". The advantage of the site was that it was to the windward of the city centre and was separated from it by the River. Unfortunately for the Lauries the scheme, begun in 1804, proved a disaster. Tolls on the two bridges over the Clyde were partly to blame, as they made access to and from the city expensive. The main reason, however, lay in the fact that the Lauries did not own all the land south of the river; nor was the south bank within the jurisdiction of the Corporation. This situation resulted in the indiscriminate use for industrial purposes of the land surrounding the development. Before half of the proposed development was under way, the area had become surrounded by mine workings and brickworks.

Further decline came in 1834 when William Dixon, who owned an iron works in the south-east of the area, drove a service rail track across the Gorbals streets to Windmill Quay in the north west. The developers were powerless to stop him. As a result, the middle class moved out to the airier suburbs in the West End. The fate of the district was sealed in the early 1840s when two main viaducted rail lines were driven through from the south on either side of the Laurie development. The decline of the area was rapid. Large houses left by the wealthy became divided internally; often single rooms were let off to entire families—a classic example of a decline into slum conditions. The down-at-heel residential area became attractive to backyard industries and service trades searching for cheap accommodation near the city centre.

The period 1850 to 1870 saw the growth of densely-packed tenement buildings. The Glasgow tenements were generally four stories in height, built in hollow rectangles following a rectangular street grid. They were executed in dressed sandstone, in many cases to quite sound architectural designs. Behind these rather grand facades, however, lay appalling housing conditions. Nearly 90% of the tenements built in the Gorbals had either one room (single end) or two rooms (room and kitchen). It was not uncommon for there to be eight separate dwellings in each storey having access from a common stair open to the street. Toilet accommodation was generally restricted to a shared W.C. on the common stair landing.

Despite the ticketing system adopted by the health authority, it was not uncommon to find families of eight or nine sharing a single end. This form of accommodation contained all facilities for the family excluding a W.C. It measured approximately $9' 6'' \times 10' 6''$ giving a floor area of around $100 \, \text{ft}^2$—about the size of a modern double bedroom. In the

Gorbals almost a third of the homes were built back to back with no through ventilation. These overcrowded and insanitary conditions were further worsened with the development of the notorious "backland" tenement. When the shortage of building land became acute, the back courts of some tenement blocks were exploited by developers who erected a single line of tenements—cut off from sunlight, daylight and fresh air. The conditions in the backland tenements were wretched.

The physical decay of the area did not come about primarily because the tenements were badly built. Part of the reason lay in the intensive use of the buildings by large numbers of closely-confined people. The main reason can be attributed to lack of maintenance by the building owners—particularly in the war years and in the depression of the 1930s. (In Glasgow the vast majority of homes were rented. The occupiers were not responsible for maintenance.) A radical improvement of these conditions did not occur until the 1950s, when the redevelopment programme began. One of the first areas to be tackled was the part of the Gorbals known as Hutchesontown—the Hutchesontown/Gorbals Comprehensive Development Area.

CDA procedure

Before the development of the Hutchesontown/Gorbals area can be discussed in detail, the reader should be aware in general terms of the procedure used in initiating and implementing a Comprehensive Development Area (CDA). It is not our purpose to deal in detail with the extraordinarily complex issues raised in the development of a CDA. The precise methods by which CDAs have been set up may vary from one local authority to another, depending on circumstances, and the techniques of redevelopment evolved in Glasgow cannot be thought to apply generally. In the ensuing paragraphs, therefore, only a brief outline has been given in order that the reader may grasp the essential principles. The sequence of events is as follows:

1. Plan preparation:
    (i) Negotiation and consultation
    (ii) Formal documents
    (iii) Approval by the Corporation
2. Statutory procedure
3. Implementation

1. Plan preparation

(i) *Negotiation and consultation*
The main work of plan preparation and subsequent implementation falls

on the Corporation Planning Department, assisted by the Town Clerk, who deals with the legalities, and the City Estates Surveyor, who handles compulsory purchase and compensation, and advises on industrial and commercial development and relocation. These three main departments are responsible through sub-committees to the Planning Committee of the Corporation, which is answerable for all major planning decisions. Other committees such as the Housing, Highways and Education committees act jointly with the Planning Committee when necessary. Thus the plans for a CDA are not carried out in isolation. Plan preparation is mainly an administrative task in which the role of the planner is that of coordinator and arbiter. Within the local authority, he has to resolve the various and often conflicting demands of other departments, frequently in competition for scarce urban land. Outside the Corporation, negotiations are conducted with statutory undertakers such as the electricity, gas and water boards, with regard to the provision of new services, and the termination or relocation of those existing. Here careful planning is required, as the relocation of main services is costly. Indeed, many CDAs have been planned around the existing street pattern to avoid such expense. Other statutory bodies are consulted: for example, the national transport undertakings for the replacing of rail and bus services, and the health authorities for the provision of health centres.

Consultation is also carried out with organizations who represent certain sectionalized interests in the lay public; for example, the churches, and associations of local traders and businessmen. Often these organizations have been formed as a direct result of the decision by the local authority to redevelop. Conspicuous by its absence is any meaningful publicity or contact with the general public or local populations affected by proposals; this aspect will be dealt with later.

In practice, this period of consultation is time-consuming. Hold-ups arise due to public bodies not being in a position to state their requirements in five or ten years' time. Organizations representing certain sections of the public often find difficulty in achieving a consensus due to their loose-knit structure.

(ii) *Formal documents*

A series of plan documents is drawn up by Corporation officials following consultation and negotiation. These documents come within the context of the City Development Plan and are treated as statutory amendments to it. Under Development Plan procedure, these amendments are subject to publication, public inquiry and government approval. The main documents are:

(a) The Survey Report
(b) The Written Statement
(c) Maps to a scale of 1:1250.

The two principal documents are (a) and (b). The Survey Report is a factual statement of existing conditions related to: land use; structural condition of buildings; population and household structure; industry; commerce; community facilities and schools. The Written Statement contains the justification for the developments and the proposals in terms of: land use zones; residential development, including house types and density; industrial development, including the relocation policy; shops and community facilities; schools; open space; roads; programming of development; areas to be designated for compulsory purchase; and the estimated redevelopment cost in terms of acquisition, demolition and development. The maps cover all these areas, and amplify them in visual form.

(iii) *Approval by the Corporation*
After the period of consultation and the drawing up of the formal documents, the latter are put before the Corporation for approval. During the entire process of plan preparation, considerable discussion takes place between the Corporation and the Scottish Development Department, who have considerable financial and planning interests in redevelopment proposals. It is the prerogative of central government to give approval for a CDA to proceed, and to provide substantial financial assistance through special grant schemes to aid development. It is doubtful whether Glasgow's redevelopment programme could have proceeded without special Government assistance.

2. Statutory procedure

Following Corporation approval of the formal plan documents, intimation is made in the national press. There is time allowed for objections both to the CDA plans and the compulsory purchase orders for the first five years of development. No CDA in Glasgow has gone forward without objections and a subsequent public inquiry. A formal objection takes the form of an appeal to the Secretary of State. It is his usual practice to hold a public inquiry at which representatives of both sides to the dispute are heard. A Reporter is appointed to take the chair at the inquiry* and a date is fixed for the hearing. After hearing evidence from both sides, the Reporter prepares a two-part report. The first part relates to the facts of the case, including the evidence brought forward. This

* In England, the Minister has a team of full-time Inspectors who carry out similar duties.

document is made public. The second part sets down the Reporter's recommendations to the Secretary of State. This document is confidential. In making a decision, the Secretary of State is not bound to accept the Reporter's recommendations. There is no right of appeal on a ministerial decision except on a point of law.

In considering the results of the inquiry, the Secretary of State is assisted by the officers of the Scottish Development Department. Certain officers have a territorial responsibility which brings them into frequent contact with planning at a local level. A ministerial decision involves consideration of the objectives of central government in the interface between local and national planning, along with the protection of the interests of the public and a local authority as expressed through the public inquiry. It has been the case that modifications to CDA proposals have been made more in the context of regional development than as a result of local pressure.

The time scale for the preparation of plans for submission to the Secretary of State, together with the statutory procedures, varies according to the size and complexity of the particular CDA. Generally, the plan preparation takes from two to three years, and the statutory procedure about one year.

3. Implementation

The physical development of the CDA takes place in five-year phases. These are agreed when the CDA is approved. Alteration to the programming of the phased development can be undertaken by the local authority without recourse to the Secretary of State. An amendment to the land use zoning of an area, however, requires statutory approval at ministerial level. During the process of implementation, the role of the Planning Department is primarily that of co-ordinating the physical development being carried out by other departments of the Corporation, external statutory bodies and private enterprise. Planning control is exercised under the normal procedure which controls all forms of development within a local authority area. In addition, the Planning Department often prepares the detailed planning requirements for individual developments being carried out under public control or privately. These Planning Briefs consider the relationship of individual developments in the planning context of the immediate environment, and stipulate conditions regarding, e.g. layout, density of development, physical form and the use of materials.

The redevelopment of the Gorbals

The first official description of the Gorbals as an area for redevelopment

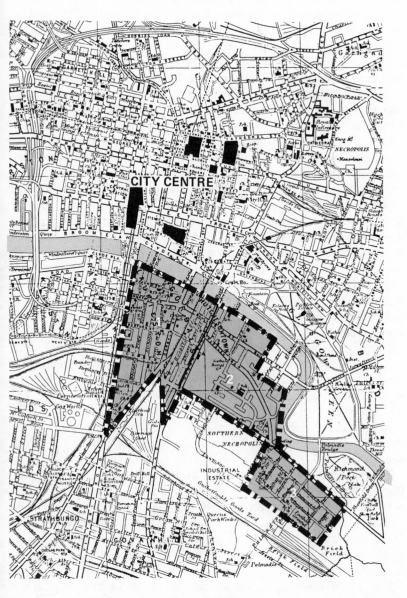

Figure 5.6   The Gorbals. Suggested area for redevelopment 1953. The three neighbour-hood units.

was made in the City's Development Plan in 1951. At that time this sector of the city was to be developed primarily for residential purposes during the 6–20 year period of the plan. This was subsequently confirmed by the approval of the Development Plan by the Secretary of State. A more detailed proposal followed in November 1953 when a Corporation Report defined the area for action. The site comprised most of the Gorbals district and extended to 342 acres (see figure 5.6); it contained 16,271 dwellings and had a total population of 55,284—slightly above the population of a large Scottish town, e.g. Kilmarnock, Clydebank or Kirkcaldy.

One of the main considerations of the Report was the question of "overspill" and housing density. These topics were closely linked. It was clearly seen that if modern standards of development were to be adopted, and overspill of population kept to a minimum, then the population density in new housing was crucial. The existing net residential density* was around 450 persons per acre, and the gross density around 162 persons per acre. The Report reckoned that, if multi-storey development were undertaken, the gross density would be 78 p.p.a. If development up to five storeys only was considered, then the gross density would be around 44 p.p.a. This would mean a difference in overspill of 11,000. It was obvious that, if the Corporation's policy of reducing overspill was to be maintained, then a considerable amount of multi-storey development would be undertaken.

One of the main obstacles to developing the district as one integrated unit was the sheer size of the area; it was concluded that the redevelopment zone would require to be broken down into manageable units within an overall planning framework. But this was not easily done. The principal inhibiting factor was the fact that the area was divided up by rigid physical barriers—several main traffic arteries giving access to the city centre from the south, and two rail lines serving the national network (see figure 5.7).

The replanning of the main traffic routes in the context of the Highway Plan would improve the situation with regard to layout, but there was no possibility of by-passing the area as a whole. Consequently, the area was divided into three neighbourhood units—eastern, central and western. These units were later to become respectively the Hutchesontown/Polmadie CDA, the Hutchesontown/Gorbals CDA and the Laurieston/Gorbals CDA.

It was proposed that the central unit be developed first. Within the overall planning framework, the Hutchesontown/Gorbals area would

---

* Net residential density refers to the number of people per acre solely in residential land use. The gross residential density refers to the number of people per acre in the entire area comprising all land uses.

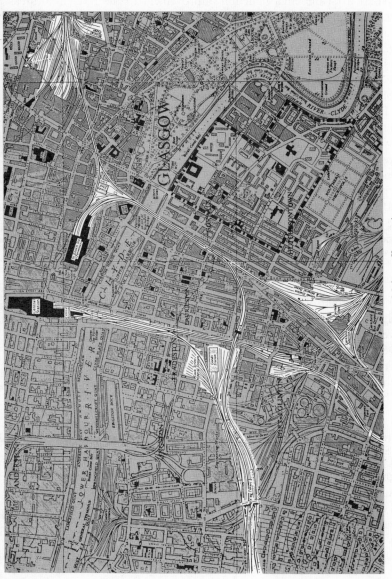

Figure 5.7   Main traffic arteries.

contain the principal facilities, such as shopping for the District as a whole.

Apart from the environmental improvement to the residential areas contained in the plan, there were spin-offs from the redevelopment process which affected areas far beyond the district being re-planned, e.g. the benefits of an improved traffic hierarchy giving better access to and from the city centre; and the reduction of atmospheric pollution by the policy of making the CDAs smokeless zones (in the Gorbals area alone this meant the elimination of some 20,000 domestic flues).

The topography of the area presented no great obstacle to redevelopment; the site was generally flat with a gentle slope from the south-west towards the river. The subsoil structure, however, presented real problems, especially with regard to multi-storey development. These bad ground conditions were made up of limestone in the north-west through Millstone Grit to formerly productive Coal Measures in the south and east. The underlying bedrock was covered with a fresh-water alluvium. This made the difficult piling work associated with multi-storey development both time-consuming and expensive.

The Hutchesontown/Gorbals CDA

By the summer of 1954 the planning process had begun for this central neighbourhood unit. In September 1955 the formal plan documents were given approval by the Corporation, who submitted them to the Secretary of State in April 1956. The public inquiry took place in September/October 1956, and final approval was given by the Government in February 1957. The total cost of development was estimated at that time to be approximately £13 million.

The old Gorbals

At the time of the Survey the defined area enclosed 111 acres (see figure 5.8). The population (based on the 1951 census) was 26,860 and the total number of families was 7,790. The net residential acreage was 58·6 acres, and the average net residential density was 458·6 p.p.a. The average number of persons per room was 1·89. Comparative figures may be seen from the following table, extracted from the 1951 census:

City	Occupancy rate	
Glasgow	1·27	persons per room
Edinburgh	0·93	,,
Newcastle	0·88	,,
Liverpool	0·83	,,
Greater London	0·77	,,
Birmingham	0·77	,,

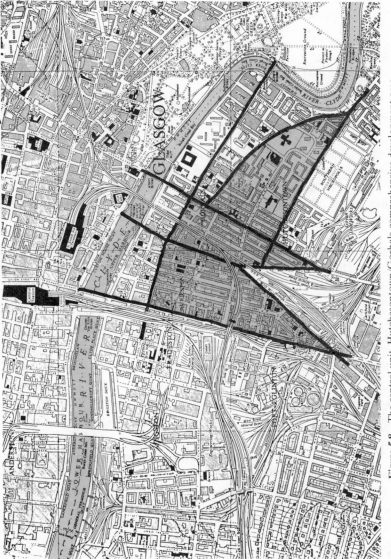

Figure 5.8   The central unit. Hutchesontown/Gorbals comprehensive development area boundary 1957.

Manchester	0·74 persons per room	
Bristol	0·72	,,
Hutchesontown/Gorbals	1·89	,,

The overcrowding and density figures were high and were more than matched by the condition of the houses, most of which were from 60 to 100 years old. The following table briefly summarizes the position:

Total number of dwellings	7,605
One and two apartment houses	87%
Back-to-back houses	33%
Houses with baths	3%
Houses with shared W.C.	78% *average* 4 families/W.C.
Houses unacceptable sanitarily	91%
Houses unacceptable structurally	95%

According to the Survey Report the area was not important industrially, only 12 firms out of a total of 105 having floor areas greater than 10,000 ft^2. The majority of the firms in the area were small, and were either service trades or performed functions ancillary to the retail trade, e.g. hosiery manufacture, and food and drink processing.

Commercial activity in the area included 444 shops and 48 pubs, together with the usual sprinkling of community services such as doctors' surgeries, post offices, cinemas, churches, library and police station. An unusual sidelight to the list of community facilities was the relatively high proportion of buildings set aside for community use. Apart from six church halls there were 15 other halls and meeting rooms.

The new Gorbals

The policy assumptions set out by the Corporation for the redeveloped area can be briefly summarized as follows:

(1) all existing industry should be removed, with the exception of the substantial long-life buildings located in the north-east sector;
(2) all existing services should be retained and utilized as far as possible;
(3) as a consequence of (2), the proposed road pattern should be based on that existing;
(4) optimum densities should be achieved.

The adequacy of these bland loosely-structured policies in relation to the formation of realistic planning objectives will be discussed later.

The redevelopment proposals may be summarized as follows:

(1) *Land use zoning*
(2) *Residential development and population*
   The first task in the preparation of the CDA proposals was the calculation of housing accommodation which would give the optimum acceptable population density compatible with national housing standards, and the provision of supporting land uses such

as schools, open space, and commercial development. The calculations made in the written statement revealed that the residential component would cover an area of 62 acres, and would accommodate 3502 dwellings housing a population of 10,179. The future population would be housed at a net residential density of 164 persons per acre. In order to achieve this, it was proposed that low-rise (up to 4 storeys) development would constitute 48·7% of development and multi-storey housing 51·3%. The proposed population figure indicated that 16,681 people had to be rehoused outwith the CDA. During the initial stages of development, in order to demolish and rebuild, it was assumed that 500 families per year would require to be rehoused. Of these, approximately 200 would be relocated within the CDA.

(3) *Industrial development*

Under the plan proposals, the only retained industry was located in a small area in the north-east sector of the CDA. Almost all other industry (whether by virtue of size, function or the type of process undertaken) was seen as incompatible with a residential area. It was proposed that 72 such firms be relocated on various sites on the periphery of the city which comprised 63 acres of land already owned by the Corporation and zoned for industrial use. Only service trades were to be relocated within the CDA, and 3 acres of ground were set aside for the purpose.

(4) *Shops and community facilities*

It was proposed that 57 shops should replace the former total of 444. These were to be located in one main and three subsidiary shopping centres. The 48 pubs were reduced to a maximum of 9, to be located in the shopping areas. Support services such as banks, post offices, and doctors' surgeries, would be accommodated as required. Sites for a cinema and community centre were provided, and it was proposed that the existing library and police station would be retained. It was also agreed that nine churches would be retained in the overall plans.

(5) *Schools*

The school population was based on the future total population and a cross-section of the existing household structures in the area. Allowance was made for the raising of the school leaving age to 16. On this basis the number of schools provided was as follows:

2 Protestant Primary Schools   7·9 acres
1 Roman Catholic Primary   4·1 „
1 Protestant Secondary School   7·0 „

Allowance was made for the provision of nursery schools.

(6)   *Open space*
      The Written Statement was vague on this subject, merely indicating
      that open space would be provided along with the residential
      development. Two small areas, one a disused burial ground and
      the other beside the river, were proposed as larger elements.

(7)   *Roads*
      The arterial and sub-arterial road proposals may be seen on figure
      5.9. The residential access roads were to follow the existing road
      pattern where possible.

(8)   *Programming*
      The programming of development was based on four stages, each
      of five years. Apart from residential development, the first phase
      included the main shopping centre, clinic, etc., and a service trades
      area, together with one local shopping centre. The second and third
      phases would incorporate the school development, and the com-
      pletion of local shopping centres and the Community Centre.

The rebuilding process 1957–1974

We have seen that the plan preparation is not carried out in isolation.
This is also true of the implementation process. The detailed design
and land requirements of new development are subject to the provisions
of Design Guides and Regulations produced by the Central Government
from time to time. For example, the internal design, layout and orientation
of housing, the provision of school playing fields and open space standards
are set out in Government publications and regulations.

Any development which receives a special grant from the Government
has to be submitted to the appropriate ministerial department for approval. In the early days of Glasgow's redevelopment programme, the
slender staff resources of the Corporation were stretched to the limit, and
it became obvious that additional help would be required. It was partly
for this reason, and partly for prestige, that the Corporation appointed
some of the city's leading architects to assist in the redevelopment process.
In the designs for the Hutchesontown/Gorbals CDA the city fathers
went further afield and appointed Professor Sir Robert Matthew and
Sir Basil Spence, two of Britain's leading architects, to assist in the
design of the first-phase residential component. The bulk of the housing
in the second and third phases of development was carried out by the
Scottish Special Housing Association. This body is a Government agency
set up to supplement the programme of local authorities with severe
housing shortages.

In general, the rebuilding of the Gorbals has taken place according

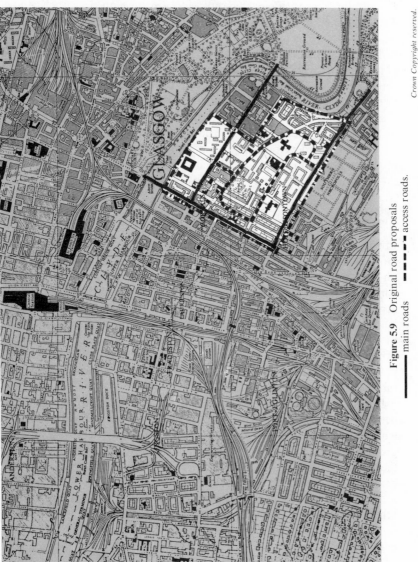

Figure 5.9 Original road proposals

━━━ main roads ━ ■ ━ ■ access roads.

to the time scale and plans contained in the written statement. There have, of course, been alterations over the last twenty years. For example, the site for a new cinema has not yet been developed as such, and a district health centre has replaced the need for doctors' surgeries. Alterations to the road pattern have taken place as a result of city-wide highway planning changes and the need to incorporate some degree of meaningful pedestrian circulation. In respect of the latter, a pedestrian walkway system has been implemented, linking all areas in the Gorbals to the central facilities in the Hutchesontown/Gorbals CDA. It is hoped that this pedestrian spine will eventually be linked with the riverside walkway along the Clyde to the north of the area. The final sector of the CDA to be developed is at present under construction in the east of the area, although lack of a clear decision on the remaining part of the city's Inner Ring Road is creating difficulties.

Community organizations

Living in the centre of a vast building site has been the lot of the Gorbals people for the last twenty years. The constant disruption of the physical environment caused by demolition and rebuilding, with their consequent dirt and noise, the frustrations caused by "temporary" arrangements for community facilities, pedestrian access, transport, etc. between phases of development, the seemingly long delays between the demolition of the old and familiar and the building and establishing of new elements within the community, have meant that the people of the Gorbals have been living under pressure for a considerable time.

Despite this, or perhaps because of it, local community groups have been particularly strong. The most significant groups in the area are the tenants' associations which were originally formed to help with housing problems. Gradually their scope has widened, and they now involve themselves with all aspects of the surrounding environment. Perhaps because of its erstwhile reputation, or the fact that it was the first CDA in Glasgow, the Gorbals has also attracted interest from voluntary and other groups from outside the area. Working together with local organizations, they have made worth-while contributions to the community in a way which was not allowed for in the original plan proposals. For example, Glasgow University in conjunction with the Corporation have given backing for a youth and community association. One of the first supervised adventure playgrounds in Glasgow was set up by a voluntary group. Local groups have converted premises as an indoor playbarn to ease the chronic shortage of play space for children.

An important factor in preserving the continuity of community life during the period of change was the decision in the plan proposals to retain most of the churches. In this way many of the original clubs and societies associated with the churches have continued in existence over the years. The single feature which best reflects the strength of the New Gorbals community is the local newspaper *The View*. This paper was established in 1967 and was the first community newspaper in Britain. It is run by and for the people of the Gorbals, and acts as their mouth-piece on important issues, as well as being a fruitful source of information on local activities. The strength of local organizations has evolved slowly over the years of change and disruption in the Gorbals. The district now has a firm base from which to operate. This will be of considerable advantage when the new Community Councils are set up under the re-organization of local government.

Change for the better?

It is singularly difficult to evaluate a programme of environmental recovery, such as the redevelopment of the Gorbals, in terms of success or failure. It would be naive to suggest that a measurement of physical achievement alone could be used to judge the results of Glasgow Corporation's mammoth attempt to re-construct the inner areas of the city. As far as the redevelopment of the Gorbals is concerned, the City authority can have a justified sense of achievement. The master plan drawn up nearly twenty years ago is almost complete: 27,000 people living in slum conditions have been rehoused in new dwellings. An attempt has been made to create in physical terms a new community by supplying a wide range of facilities not found in many large housing schemes and by creating a physical environment of a high design standard and layout.

It is, however, almost impossible to assess the effect on a community of thousands which has been subject to decimation and continual upheaval in the redevelopment process. The physical artifacts of redevelopment are important in terms of the creation of quality and character in the environment, but they take second place to what planned redevelopment is about, namely people. Just as it is impossible to gauge the real effects of breaking up a community which had evolved over a period of a hundred years, with its sophisticated interrelationships of social structure, so it is equally futile to judge the success of the New Gorbals at this moment.

From a planning point of view, the Glasgow CDA programme has not been wholly effective. This is partly due to the legislation by which redevelopment was undertaken, and partly to the time involved in carrying out projects. Of the twenty-nine CDAs proposed in 1957, only nine have been approved, and there are two awaiting approval by the Secretary of State. Once again, planning has been overtaken by events: over the last decade public opinion has changed considerably, and new attitudes to the problems of urban areas have brought about a significant change in planning and housing legislation. It is now no longer possible to carry out redevelopment on the scale and in the manner adopted by Glasgow in the 1950s. The criticisms of the CDA method of redevelopment were mainly directed at the rigidity with which the 1947 Act was interpreted both by Government and local authorities. There was also considerable doubt as to the efficacy of developing large areas of cities over considerable periods of time, with constant disruption to community life. The fact that the land use zonings of the 1947 Act were used rigidly as prime controls in the redevelopment programme and that the boundaries of CDAs were tightly drawn and virtually unalterable once approved, meant that the plans were inflexible. Generally, they were slow to cope with the continual change in new ideas and attitudes to the restructuring of urban areas. Such criticism may be applied to Glasgow's CDA programme and to the redevelopment of the Gorbals. The original report on the Gorbals area proposed that development should take place in three sections. To date only the central unit (Hutchesontown/Gorbals) is reaching completion. The plans for the western unit (Laurieston/Gorbals) were approved in 1966, almost a decade after the development of the entire area had begun. This area will not be complete until well after 1980. The third sector (the Hutchesontown/Polmadie CDA) has been dropped from the comprehensive development programme.

The very loose planning objectives defined in the written statements of the western and central sectors of the Gorbals area have not produced an integrated framework allowing development to take place over a long time. Adherence to a rigid interpretation of legislation, particularly with regard to land use zonings, has resulted in development taking place in isolated unrelated compartments. There has also been a lack of flexibility in land use to accommodate the changing social needs of the emerging community. In the city as a whole we have seen that the original CDA proposals were often linked with the city Highway Plan. In this sense, the CDAs have been integrated into the strategic planning of the city. Because of tightly drawn boundaries, however, they have often failed to become integrated with surrounding new or established areas. They tend to stand out as isolated pockets of development.

Criticism, however justified, is easy with hindsight. The problems which the city faced in the immediate post-war period have been tackled assiduously by the local authority. Since 1959 the population of the inner city areas has been substantially cleared and considerable rebuilding has taken place.

As previously mentioned, much of the criticism of CDA procedure and of planning in general has been laid at the door of post-war legislation. Criticism of the inadequacies of the existing legislation was, however, not the only factor which eventually brought about a fundamental change in Government planning policies. The attitudes in society towards the problems of living in urban areas in a period of rapid change had been changing since the end of the war. For example, planning as a discipline in its own right had begun to emerge. The majority of those who were involved with the operation of the post-war legislation were architects, engineers and surveyors who had only minimal training in planning. It is not surprising, therefore, that planning problems were seen mainly in terms of the physical environment.

By the early 1960s, the base of the planning profession had been considerably broadened; new undergraduate courses in planning brought many into local authorities who had a much wider theoretical knowledge of the subject; new expertise was gained by the addition of geographers, economists and sociologists to the staffs of many planning departments. The change to a more theoretical interdisciplinary approach resulted in movement away from physical land-use planning to the consideration of urban problems in social and economic terms. Another aspect of the change in thinking which was to influence future legislation was the growing awareness by the public that it was being increasingly affected by major planning decisions over which it had little or no control. Pressure gradually mounted for change which would bring about increased participation by the public in planning decisions.

In the mid 1960s, the Government commissioned two Reports which were to become instruments for change in legislation. The first of these ("The Future of Development Plans", 1965) recommended wide-ranging changes in planning legislation. The main intent of the Report was to separate, as part of the planning process, strategic decisions and tactical decisions. It also recommended that ministerial involvement in the planning process should be kept to a minimum, and should be reserved only for major strategic issues. The policy content of plans would be strengthened, and the range of planning activity would be widened in economic and social terms to provide an integrated planning framework from regional to local level. The Report also suggested that the CDA procedure should be discontinued and replaced with a much more flexible and less-time-consuming system.

The second Report ("People and Planning", 1969) dealt with the concept of public participation in planning, and outlined in considerable detail a mechanism for public consultation at each stage of the plan-making process. In producing the major planning and housing legislation of 1968/69, the Government incorporated the principal recommendations of both Reports. In the new planning legislation, the planning process has been divided into a two-tier system of Structure Planning and Local Planning.

Structure Plans are statements of general policy, aims and objectives in the context of the social and economic environment. Maps, which were the cornerstone of previous legislation, are now used only to illustrate the policy document: they indicate broad land use policies without any reference to detailed land-use zonings. The Structure Plan document must be statutorily approved by the Government, and evidence must be given of public consultation during all stages of the plan preparation. The broad strategies embodied in the Structure Plan imply that plan making will be carried out in terms of the total environment, in a way which will make a more rational use of scarce resources.

The second tier in the new system is local planning. Local plans are subject only to the approval of the local authority and, although they may not be prepared until a Structure Plan has been approved, they offer wide scope for the local authority to speed up the planning process and to initiate change without constant reference to agencies of central government. This new loose-fit plan type is much more flexible than the old development plan approach.

Under the new system, the CDA approach to urban renewal was abandoned, and the process of declaring "action areas" was adopted. These areas may be defined on a local plan for either improvement or redevelopment. They are generally expected to be much smaller than the CDAs, and all development is required to be completed within a ten-year period.

In the context of the improvement of the older areas of cities, the decision to include improvement or rehabilitation along with redevelopment is important. One of the major disadvantages of the CDA programme was that it was time-consuming, disruptive to community life and, above all, expensive. It often removed fit houses along with the unfit, efficient businesses along with the inefficient, for the sake of the overall master plan. In the light of prevailing economic circumstances, and in the growing awareness of the sensitive structure of local economics and communities, the emphasis is now placed firmly on improvement rather than redevelopment. Planners are now using toothpicks rather than bull-dozers to effect their plans.

Conclusions

We have seen how the basis for really meaningful reclamation of the decayed environments of the inner areas of our cities evolved through gradual social and political change, and was subject to the vagaries of the prevailing economic climate. The pattern of change in urban society has become increasingly rapid over the last thirty years; the rather rigid paternalistic and costly approach to urban renewal has given way to what we now believe is a more realistic, sensitive and enlightened approach. Although the CDA policies for environmental recovery were not the universal panacea hoped for, they played a vital role in the improvement of the physical environment for a large section of the urban population. Cities such as Glasgow which have courageously undertaken the transformation of the physical environment may have paved the way for new techniques in environmental reclamation.

FURTHER READING

Abercrombie (1946), Clyde Valley Regional Plan, H.M.S.O.

The Artizan, October 1843, p. 229, col. 2.

City of Glasgow, First Development Plan Survey Report, 1951.

The Future of Development Plans (1965), The Planning Advisory Group, H.M.S.O.

People and Planning, Report by the Skeffington Committee, H.M.S.O., 1969

Report of the Royal Commission on the Housing of the Industrial Population of Scotland, Rural and Urban (1917), H.M.S.O., Edinburgh.

Planning our New Homes (1943), The Scottish Housing Advisory Committee Report, H.M.S.O.

J. C. Symonds (1839), Report of the Royal Commission on Handloom Weavers, Parliamentary Papers, Vol. 42, No. 159, p. 51.

Index